Bridge by Question and Answer

Terence Reese

Bridge by Question and Answer

Arthur Barker Limited   London
A subsidiary of Weidenfeld (Publishers) Limited

Published in Great Britain by
Arthur Barker Limited
11 St John's Hill   London SW11

ISBN 0 213 16583 X

Filmset by Keyspools Limited, Golborne, Lancs.
Printed in Great Britain by Morrison & Gibb Limited,
Edinburgh.

Contents

Foreword

Some problems provide mental stimulus but have little relevance to practical play; others illustrate varied forms of technique. I have aimed mostly at the second kind. The test of such a problem is that a fairly experienced player should say, 'I ought to have got that; next time, I will.'

The rough division into chapters enables the reader, if he so wishes, to study a group of problems which have the same general theme. It is a good way of learning, I think. Of course, to know the theme of a problem is an aid to the solver. Anyone who disdains such assistance is welcome to open the book at random.

The 'preliminary analysis' which follows each question may help the reader to order his thoughts in a logical way. The analysis sets the problem in focus but does not foretell the answer.

One acknowledgement I must certainly make is to Alan Hiron, who has supplied me with many excellent hands over the years. It is quite possible that, without knowing it, I owe a debt to other writers. Good problems, like comedians' jokes, quickly go the rounds and their origins are soon lost.

TERENCE REESE

How to use this book

Each problem in this book appears on a right hand page. Its solution can be found on the left hand page overleaf. The problems are arranged thematically but no indication of the theme appears beyond the Contents page.

Dealer, North   *Game all*

             ♠ A Q 2
             ♡ 5 2
             ◇ A Q 8 6 5 4
             ♣ 10 6

♠ 3 led

             ♠ K 10 8 7
             ♡ Q 9 7 4
             ◇ K 9
             ♣ A J 5

The bidding

South	West	North	East
—	—	1 ◇	pass
1 ♡ (1)	pass	2 ◇	pass
3NT	pass	pass	pass

Final contract – 3NT

(1) With 4–4 in the majors it is normal to respond in the lower valued suit, so that a fit in the other major will not be lost.

The lead
West leads the 3 of spades. How should South plan the play?

Preliminary analysis
No problem, obviously, if the diamonds are 3–2; if not, there are only eight tricks on top and a possible danger of losing a diamond and four hearts.

The worst that can happen here (barring a 5–0 break in diamonds) is that East will win a diamond trick and lead a heart through declarer. It is possible, in that case, to lose four heart tricks. For example, East might lead a low heart from A x x and find his partner with K J 10 x, or the distribution might be like this:

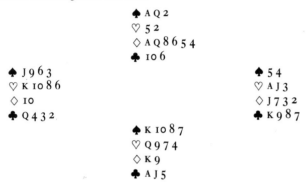

If East is allowed to win a diamond he will switch to the jack of hearts and set up four tricks in this suit. On the other hand, if West wins a diamond trick there is no distribution of hearts which will enable the defenders to take four quick tricks.

As three tricks in spades will be enough, and he wants to make an avoidance play in diamonds, South should go up with the ace of spades at trick one and play a low diamond, inserting the 9. This loses to the 10, but the defence can take only three heart tricks and South makes game with three spades, five diamonds and one club.

If South makes the mistake of letting the first spade run to the 10 in his own hand, he cannot follow this line of play.

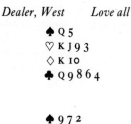

Dealer, West   Love all

♠ Q 5
♡ K J 9 3
◇ K 10
♣ Q 9 8 6 4

♠ 6 led

♠ 9 7 2
♡ A Q 10 8 6
◇ J 4
♣ A J 10

The bidding

South	West	North	East
—	pass	pass	pass
1 ♡	pass	3 ♡	pass
pass (1)	pass		

Final contract – Three Hearts

(1) South should be happy to make a part score after opening fourth in hand.

The lead

West leads the 6 of spades, East wins with the ace and returns the 3. West takes this trick with the king and exits with the 3 of diamonds. How should South plan the play?

Preliminary analysis

Declarer's play to this trick may be critical. Having reflected on the bidding and future prospects, should he play the king of diamonds or the 10 – and why?

In a situation of this sort, where there is another finesse to follow, declarer should consider not only how he *expects* the cards to lie, but how he *wants* them to lie.

The superficial view here is to say, 'East had the ace of spades, so I will play for the aces to be divided.' To go up with the king of diamonds loses the contract when the cards are like this:

```
                   ♠ Q 5
                   ♡ K J 9 3
                   ◇ K 10
                   ♣ Q 9 8 6 4
  ♠ K J 8 6                          ♠ A 10 4 3
  ♡ 7 5                              ♡ 4 2
  ◇ Q 9 5 3                          ◇ A 8 7 6 2
  ♣ K 7 5                            ♣ 3 2
                   ♠ 9 7 2
                   ♡ A Q 10 8 6
                   ◇ J 4
                   ♣ A J 10
```

Having taken the wrong view in diamonds, South goes one down, losing two spades, two diamonds and a club.

Note that there is nothing implausible in the lay-out above. But suppose declarer takes the other view and finesses ◇ 10, losing to the queen: what will happen to him then?

The answer is that if West has the ace of diamonds and East the queen, then surely the club finesse will be right. West is already marked with four spades to the king, probably king-jack. Give him the ace of diamonds and the king of clubs, and he would have had something to say over one heart, having passed originally.

So South says to himself, 'I don't mind if the 10 loses to the queen, because then the club finesse will be right and I shall still make the contract.'

Another way of saying the same thing: South mentally places West with the king of clubs. Having made that assumption, he is inclined to place East with the ace of diamonds.

Dealer, West *N–S vulnerable*

♠ K 10 5
♡ K 10 7 4
♢ 8 4 2
♣ A 9 5

♢ A led

♠ A Q J 4
♡ A Q 6
♢ Q 9 5
♣ 8 6 3

The bidding

South	West	North	East
—	1 ♢	pass	1 ♡
1 ♠ (1)	pass	2 ♠	pass
2NT	pass	3NT	pass
pass	pass		

Final contract – 3NT

(1) The best alternative, at the score, is to pass, rather than bid 1NT or double.

The lead

West leads the ace of diamonds and East drops the 6. West switches to the 7 of clubs. How should South plan the play?

Preliminary analysis

Inquiry reveals that West's lead of the ace of diamonds asks partner to drop an honour or the highest card from three. South is looking at eight top tricks, but unless West has a singleton jack of hearts it is not easy to see where the ninth will come from.

Declarer must obviously go up with the ace of clubs, as he cannot risk letting East in to lead a diamond through the queen.

One possibility is to play off the winning spades and hearts, hoping for an end-play against West; but it shouldn't be difficult for West to avoid this, even if he has the king of clubs, which is not certain. The hand in fact was:

```
                    ♠ K 10 5
                    ♡ K 10 7 4
                    ◇ 8 4 2
                    ♣ A 9 5
  ♠ 9 7 6 3                          ♠ 8 2
  ♡ 8                                ♡ J 9 5 3 2
  ◇ A K J 10 3                       ◇ 7 6
  ♣ Q 10 7                           ♣ K J 4 2
                    ♠ A Q J 4
                    ♡ A Q 6
                    ◇ Q 9 5
                    ♣ 8 6 3
```

There is a hidden trick here. After the ace of clubs declarer should lead the 10 of hearts from dummy, aiming to pin a singleton 8 or 9 in the West hand. (If West's singleton is the jack, too bad!) As the cards lie, there are just enough entries for South to make four heart tricks. East covers the 10 with the Jack, and the 8 falls under the ace. South returns to the 10 of spades, finesses the 6 of hearts, cashes the queen, and still has the king of spades as an entry to the table.

Dealer, South   Love all

♠ Q 7 5 4
♡ A
◇ K J
♣ A J 10 8 7 2

♡ K led

♠ A K J
♡ J 9
◇ A 7 6 5
♣ Q 6 5 3

The bidding

South	West	North	East
1 ◇	1 ♠	2 ♣	pass
2NT (1)	pass	3NT	pass
pass	pass		

Final contract – 3NT

(1) Not the happiest of choices, as it turns out, but most players would do the same at this point.

The lead
West leads the king of hearts and East plays the 3. How should South plan the play?

Preliminary analysis
South notes unhappily that if 3NT can be made, so can seven clubs. At no trumps, eight tricks are in sight, whatever the situation in clubs. What is the best chance to arrive at a ninth?

It looks at first as though South can combine the chances in diamonds and clubs by playing off the ace of clubs and, if the king does not fall, finessing the jack of diamonds.

Closer inspection reveals that there is an entry problem. If South follows the ace of hearts with the ace of clubs, and the king does not appear, he cannot make three tricks in diamonds and four in spades, even if the queen of diamonds is on the right side for him. Whatever the order of play, one suit or the other will be blocked.

There remains one small extra chance: play to drop a singleton queen of diamonds and reap the reward of virtue when the cards lie like this:

```
                      ♠ Q 7 5 4
                      ♡ A
                      ◇ K J
                      ♣ A J 10 8 7 2
♠ 10 9 8 6 3 2                          ♠ —
♡ K Q 10 6 2                            ♡ 8 7 5 4 3
◇ Q                                     ◇ 10 9 8 4 3 2
♣ 9                                     ♣ K 4
                      ♠ A K J
                      ♡ J 9
                      ◇ A 7 6 5
                      ♣ Q 6 5 3
```

South plays the king of diamonds at trick two and when the queen falls he can run nine tricks without taking the club finesse.

Dealer, East   Love all

             ♠ A J 7 4 2
             ♡ Q 10
             ◇ A K 4
             ♣ 8 4 3

♣ 5 led

             ♠ 9 3
             ♡ J 7 6 5 3
             ◇ 10 5 2
             ♣ A K J

The bidding

South	West	North	East
—	—	—	1 ♣
pass	pass	dble	pass
1 ♡	pass	1 ♠	pass
2NT (1)	pass	3NT (2)	pass
pass	pass		

Final contract – 3NT

(1) It is close whether South should bid 1NT or 2NT at this point.

(2) North, also, is pushing a little, but he knows it is often possible to make 3NT with minimum values when all the opposing strength is in one hand.

The lead

West leads the 5 of clubs, East plays the queen, and South wins with the ace. As he will need at least one trick in hearts even if spades are 3–3, South leads a heart to the queen. East wins with the king and plays a second club, on which West plays the 7. How should South continue?

Preliminary analysis

It looks as though the clubs are 4–3. As opponents are playing a weak no trump, East is probably outside the range for 1NT and has 15 or 16 points. South has six tricks on top and can make at least one more in hearts. He will still need to develop one of the major suits.

There is a neat point in this hand, which for some reason seldom finds its way into bridge literature.

```
                        ♠ A J 7 4 2
                        ♡ Q 10
                        ◇ A K 4
                        ♣ 8 4 3
        ♠ 10 8 5                          ♠ K Q 6
        ♡ 9 8 4                           ♡ A K 2
        ◇ J 8 7 6                         ◇ Q 9 3
        ♣ 10 7 5                          ♣ Q 9 6 2
                        ♠ 9 3
                        ♡ J 7 6 5 3
                        ◇ 10 5 2
                        ♣ A K J
```

The play began with a club to the ace, a heart to the queen and king, and a club to the king. South now led a heart to the 10, which was allowed to hold. Short of entries to establish the hearts, declarer turned to spades. East won with the queen and led a third club. The best that South could do now was clear the spades; meanwhile, the defence took five tricks by way of two spades, two hearts and a club.

A slight change in the order of play wins the contract. South should foresee that East will not capture the second heart. The solution is to cross to the ace of diamonds and lead the 10 of hearts from the table. Now, if East ducks, South can overtake with the jack and clear the suit.

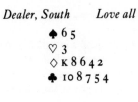

Dealer, South   *Love all*

♠ 6 5
♡ 3
◇ K 8 6 4 2
♣ 10 8 7 5 4

♠ Q led

♠ A K
♡ A K 5
◇ J 9 5
♣ A J 9 3 2

The bidding

South	West	North	East
1 ♣	1 ♠	2 ♣	2 ♠
3NT	pass	pass (1)	pass

Final contract – 3NT

(1) Not caring for it overmuch, but he is not in the driving seat.

The lead

West leads the queen of spades, East plays the 7 and South wins with the king. How should he plan the play?

Preliminary analysis

It is unlikely that the clubs are 3–0, so to play on clubs at once will probably establish eight tricks. Should South accept one down, or should he try to slip through a diamond?

As he is not vulnerable and not doubled, South should certainly try any reasonable play for the contract.

It may seem at first that to lead a low diamond at trick two is a forlorn chance, for West will know from the bidding that South has a club suit in reserve, together with the top spades and hearts. He will take the ace of diamonds quickly and clear the spades, hoping that declarer's clubs are not solid.

When this hand was first published it was noted that the jack of diamonds at trick two would establish sufficient tricks in diamonds when East held the singleton 10.

```
                        ♠ 6 5
                        ♡ 3
                        ◇ K 8 6 4 2
                        ♣ 10 8 7 5 4
     ♠ Q J 9 4 2                          ♠ 10 8 7 3
     ♡ J 8 2                               ♡ Q 10 9 7 6 4
     ◇ A Q 7 3                             ◇ 10
     ♣ K                                   ♣ Q 6
                        ♠ A K
                        ♡ A K 5
                        ◇ J 9 5
                        ♣ A J 9 3 2
```

Having won the first spade, South leads the jack of diamonds. If West plays low, declarer wins the trick and switches to clubs; if West takes the ace of diamonds, subsequent finesses will produce game by way of four diamonds, two spades, two hearts and a club.

The 9 of diamonds at trick two will also be good enough as the cards lie, and there are other positions where the diamond lead may win by force. Suppose that East has a singleton queen of diamonds or a doubleton Q 10. Once again, if West ducks when the jack or 9 is led, the king of diamonds will be the ninth trick, and if West plays the ace on the first round South may read the position correctly and bring in the rest of the suit.

Dealer, South   N–S vulnerable

♠ A 9 7
♡ A K 9 6 2
◇ 8 6 4 2
♣ 7

♣ K led

♠ K Q J 10 8 5
♡ J 10 7
◇ K 10
♣ A 4

The bidding

South	West	North	East
1 ♠	2NT (1)	3 ♣ (2)	4 ♣
4 ♠	5 ♣	5 ♠	pass
pass	pass		

Final contract – Five Spades

(1) This is the 'unusual notrump', signifying length in both minor suits.

(2) North uses a sophisticated counter. By bidding three clubs, a suit the opponents are known to hold, he indicates good values, together with a shortage in clubs.

The lead
West leads the king of clubs and South wins with the ace. How should South plan the play?

Preliminary analysis
No doubt the ace of diamonds is over the king and the heart finesse is probably wrong as well. Is there any other chance?

At the table South ruffed his losing club, drew trumps, and took the heart finesse. When this lost to the queen and a diamond came back, he blamed his partner for not taking a comfortable penalty from five clubs.

Examination of the cards revealed that declarer had missed a slender but legitimate chance.

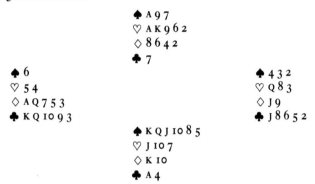

If the heart queen is coming down, South will always make the contract, so it can hardly cost to play diamonds first. South ruffs a club at trick two and leads a low diamond, covering the 9 with the 10. Later the king forces the ace from West and the jack from East, leaving dummy's 8 a master.

There is one other theoretical chance, it is true. If East has the queen of diamonds single it will be safe to give him a heart trick, as the diamonds will be blocked.

Dealer, South   *Game all*

            ♠ J 10 7
            ♡ A 5
            ◇ 10 8 2
            ♣ A K 7 5 3

♡ 10 led

            ♠ A 2
            ♡ Q 4 3
            ◇ K Q J 3
            ♣ 10 8 6 4

The bidding

South	West	North	East
1NT (1)	pass	3NT	pass
pass	pass		

Final contract – 3NT

(1) Not everyone's choice for a vulnerable notrump, but it is fashionable in the tournament world to play 12–14 throughout.

The lead

On the lead of the 10 of hearts dummy plays low and East puts on the jack, which is headed by South's queen. How should South plan the play?

Preliminary analysis

After winning with the queen of hearts declarer has five tricks on top and can surely develop three in diamonds. He may also expect to develop either two or three tricks in clubs. But unless clubs are 2–2 he will have to lose a trick in each minor suit before he can arrive at nine tricks, and meanwhile the hearts are a danger. The spades, also, are open to attack if East has the lead.

In a world championship match the declarer made the reflex play of attacking diamonds at trick two. He was out of luck, not just because he lost the contract, but because the cards lay in the precise position that refuted his line of play.

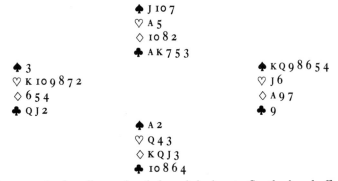

East won the first diamond and cleared the hearts. South played off his diamond winners and tried ace and king of clubs. When he found that West controlled this suit he was held to eight tricks.

The first play on this hand should be the ace and king of clubs (unblocking the 8 from hand). If it turns out that West holds the clubs, then the third club must be played before a diamond; that wins the contract as the cards lie. If it turns out instead that East holds the clubs, declarer must attack diamonds next.

It is a deceptive hand, but if you test the different possibilities you will find that it cannot cost to play on clubs first.

Dealer, South   Game all

♠ J 8 7 2
♡ J 10 4
◇ A 9
♣ K 10 8 6

♡ 6 led

♠ A Q 6
♡ K 9 5
◇ K 7 4 3
♣ A J 9

The bidding

South	West	North	East
1 NT	pass	3NT (1)	pass
pass	pass		

Final contract – 3NT

(1) North might have bid a Stayman two clubs, but when it is doubtful whether in any event the major suit will be the better contract, a raise to 3NT is usually better tactics.

The lead

West leads the 6 of hearts. Declarer goes up with dummy's jack, which holds the trick, East dropping the 8. How should South plan the play?

Preliminary analysis

It looks as though West began with five or six diamonds to the A Q. Clearly it would be dangerous to let East into the lead. Which suit should South play first?

Following two general principles – develop your best suit and attack the danger hand – South ran the 10 of clubs from dummy at trick two, losing to the queen.

South expected West to retain his heart tenace and try to put his partner in the lead, but it didn't go like that.

```
                        ♠ J 8 7 2
                        ♡ J 10 4
                        ◇ A 9
                        ♣ K 10 8 6
    ♠ K 5 3                                 ♠ 10 9 4
    ♡ A Q 7 6 2                             ♡ 8 3
    ◇ J 8 6                                 ◇ Q 10 5 2
    ♣ Q 4                                   ♣ 7 5 3 2
                        ♠ A Q 6
                        ♡ K 9 5
                        ◇ K 7 4 3
                        ♣ A J 9
```

When he won with the queen of clubs West, realizing that his partner was unlikely to have an entry card, smartly played off the ace and queen of hearts. South made his remaining clubs, West discarding a spade and a diamond. There was nothing for it but the spade finesse, and South finished one down, losing three hearts, a spade and a club.

Declarer tackled the black suits in the wrong order. Suppose he finesses the queen of spades at trick two. If West plays passively South can take the club finesse into his hand as before, and the spade break will give him nine tricks. If West, when in with the king of spades, clears his heart suit, then South can take the club finesse in the other direction, knowing that East has no more hearts.

It would be good play, admittedly, for West to let the queen of spades hold; if South missed the position he might go down.

Dealer, North   Game all

♠ Q 4
♡ A K J 8 3
◇ K 9 5 2
♣ A 6

♠ 6 led

♠ A 8 5
♡ 6 5 2
◇ A J 6 3
♣ 9 7 4

The bidding

South	West	North	East
—	—	1 ♡	pass
1 NT	pass	2NT (1)	pass
3NT	pass	No	pass

Final contract – 3NT

(1) This is the normal rebid with 17–18 points. It is true that a 5–4–2–2 hand will often play better in a suit contract, even when partner is fairly balanced, but North has values in both his short suits; also, there is room for responder, if he has three hearts and a doubleton, to bid three hearts over 2NT.

The lead
West leads the 6 of spades. Declarer goes up with dummy's queen and is happy to see it hold the trick, East dropping the 9. How should South plan the play?

Preliminary analysis
Since the queen of spades has held, four tricks in hearts will produce game. If the hearts fail, four tricks in diamonds will be enough. South must form a plan to cover the development of both these suits.

As four tricks from either red suit will be enough for game, declarer must aim to combine the chances in the best possible way.

First, he sees that the entry situation will enable him to make four heart tricks when West holds Q 10 x x. He can cash the ace and king. If East shows out on the second round declarer can come to hand with the ace of diamonds and lead up to ♡ J 8 3, ensuring four tricks in hearts plus two diamonds, two spades and one club.

Suppose, however, that East turns up with four hearts to the queen. Now South must look to the diamonds, and the diamond combination presents one of the lesser known safety plays. Four tricks can be made if East holds Q x or Q x x or singleton queen. There is no advantage in laying down the king first. In effect, declarer plays to make the contract against this distribution:

```
                    ♠ Q 4
                    ♡ A K J 8 3
                    ◊ K 9 5 2
                    ♣ A 6
   ♠ K 10 7 6 2                      ♠ J 9 3
   ♡ 4                               ♡ Q 10 9 7
   ◊ 10 8 7 4                        ◊ Q
   ♣ K 8 2                           ♣ Q J 10 5 3
                    ♠ A 8 5
                    ♡ 6 5 2
                    ◊ A J 6 3
                    ♣ 9 7 4
```

After the queen of spades has won the first trick, South lays down ace and king of hearts, West discarding a club. Seeing that the hearts will not produce enough tricks, South leads a low diamond from dummy and has no difficulty then in making four tricks in diamonds. To play the king of diamonds first would be a mistake, because even if it dropped a singleton queen in the West hand there would be no direct way of making four tricks in diamonds.

Dealer, East   Love all

        ♠ 5
        ♡ Q 8 6 3
        ◇ J 9 4
        ♣ A K Q 6 2

♠ 3 led

        ♠ Q 10 7 2
        ♡ A 7
        ◇ A Q 10 8 7
        ♣ 8 4

The bidding

South	West	North	East
—	—	—	1 ♠
2 ◇	2 ♠	3 ♠ (1)	pass
3NT	pass	pass	pass

Final contract – 3NT

(1) After his partner has overcalled at the two level, North issues a strong invitation to game. He is still free to pass four diamonds.

The lead

West leads the 3 of spades. East wins with the ace and returns the 6. How should South plan the play?

Preliminary analysis

Declarer's play to the present trick may well be decisive. West may have led from J x x of spades, East holding A K x x x; or West may hold K x x and East A J x x x. Which view should South take?

If there are no special considerations, it is generally correct to play the 10 in this well-known situation. (The reason is tied up with the 'principle of restricted choice': with A K x x x East might have played the king on the first trick instead of the ace.)

Being familiar with this argument, which applies to many guessing situations, South put in the 10. This did not turn out well, for the full hand was:

```
                    ♠ 5
                    ♡ Q 8 6 3
                    ◇ J 9 4
                    ♣ A K Q 6 2
  ♠ J 9 3                             ♠ A K 8 6 4
  ♡ 9 5 4                             ♡ K J 10 2
  ◇ K 2                               ◇ 6 5 3
  ♣ J 10 7 5 3                        ♣ 9
                    ♠ Q 10 7 2
                    ♡ A 7
                    ◇ A Q 10 8 7
                    ♣ 8 4
```

When West won the second trick with the jack of spades he switched smartly to the 9 of hearts. This led to the defence taking two hearts, three spades and a diamond.

No one can help making a wrong guess, but here South made a bad guess. He should have reasoned along these lines:

'If I put in the 10 of spades and it loses to the jack, West may switch to a heart. Suppose, instead, that I put up the queen of spades and that this loses to the king. In that case East must hold the king of diamonds for his opening bid and I shall have at least nine tricks on top.'

Dealer, South   Game all

         ♠ K J 6
         ♡ K 9 4
         ◇ 7 5 2
         ♣ J 9 5 4

◇ K led

         ♠ A Q 9
         ♡ A 10 8 6 5 2
         ◇ J 8
         ♣ A Q

The bidding

South	West	North	East
1 ♡	pass	1 NT	pass
3 ♡ (1)	pass	4 ♡	pass
pass	pass		

Final contract – Four Hearts

(1) South has a powerful hand but needs some support for hearts before he can be confident of game.

The lead

West leads the king of diamonds and follows with a low diamond to his partner's ace. East returns a diamond, which South ruffs. How should South plan the play?

Preliminary analysis

South has lost two diamond tricks and must avoid losing two tricks in hearts and clubs combined. He has to decide on the best sequence of play.

There is a well-known safety play to avoid losing two tricks with K 9 4 opposite A 10 8 6 5 2: declarer plays low from one hand or the other and covers the card played by second hand.

However, it would be foolish to make the safety play in trumps, then find that hearts were 2–2 and the club finesse wrong.

Equally, it would be foolish to neglect the safety play and find that the club finesse was right, as here:

```
                    ♠ K J 6
                    ♡ K 9 4
                    ◇ 7 5 2
                    ♣ J 9 5 4
   ♠ 8 5                              ♠ 10 7 4 3 2
   ♡ Q J 7 3                          ♡ —
   ◇ K Q 10 4                         ◇ A 9 6 3
   ♣ 10 7 6                           ♣ K 8 3 2
                    ♠ A Q 9
                    ♡ A 10 8 6 5 2
                    ◇ J 8
                    ♣ A Q
```

Suppose that South, after ruffing the third diamond, plays a low heart to the king; when East shows out he finds that he must lose two trump tricks.

The answer is that South should enter dummy with a spade and test the club finesse before touching trumps. If the club finesse wins he can make the safety play in trumps; if it loses, he must do the best he can to avoid losing any trump trick.

Dealer, North   *Love all*

♠ A Q 5
♡ A 5 2
♢ 10 8 7 4 3
♣ J 10

♡ 4 led

♠ 9 3
♡ —
♢ A 9 2
♣ A K Q 9 7 6 5 2

The bidding

South	West	North	East
—	—	pass	pass
1 ♣	pass	1 ♢	2 ♣
5 ♣ (1)	pass	6 ♣ (2)	pass
pass	pass		

Final contract – Six Clubs

(1) As East's two clubs, following his original pass, is obviously based on a pronounced major two-suiter, it must be sensible to pre-empt to the limit.

(2) North is aware that his poor diamonds are a drawback, as no doubt South has some diamond fit, but the two aces and the J 10 of clubs must pull some weight.

The lead

West leads the 4 of hearts. How should South plan the play?

Preliminary analysis

South has eleven tricks on top. He cannot be hopeful of the spade finesse, but as one of his diamonds can be discarded on the ace of hearts, perhaps something can be done with this suit?

The obvious line is to go up with the ace of hearts, discarding a diamond, and then play ace and another diamond. This would be good enough if diamonds were 3–2 and clubs 2–1.

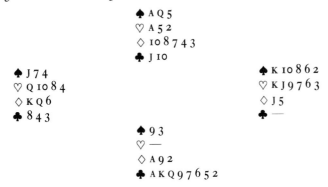

                    ♠ A Q 5
                    ♡ A 5 2
                    ◇ 10 8 7 4 3
                    ♣ J 10
    ♠ J 7 4   ♠ K 10 8 6 2
    ♡ Q 10 8 4   ♡ K J 9 7 6 3
    ◇ K Q 6   ◇ J 5
    ♣ 8 4 3   ♣ —
                    ♠ 9 3
                    ♡ —
                    ◇ A 9 2
                    ♣ A K Q 9 7 6 5 2

South goes up with ace of hearts, discarding a diamond, then plays ace and another diamond. West wins and attacks spades. If declarer plays the ace, ruffs a diamond, and returns to the 10 of clubs, he is defeated by the (not unexpected) break in trumps.

The solution is pretty. Making absolutely sure, South covers the 4 of hearts with the 5 at trick one, then lets East hold the trick! East cannot attack the spades to good purpose. Say that he returns a heart. South ruffs, cashes ace of diamonds, and crosses to the jack of clubs. His last diamond goes away on the ace of hearts and a diamond is ruffed; then back to 10 of clubs, another diamond ruff, and the ace of spades is still in dummy as an entry for the long diamonds.

Dealer, North   Game all

    ♠ K 10 4
    ♡ Q J 9
    ◇ K J 10 8 3
    ♣ A 6

♣ J led

    ♠ A J 5
    ♡ K 10 8 7 3
    ◇ Q 9 4
    ♣ 9 5

The bidding

South	West	North	East
—	—	1 ◇	pass
1 ♡	pass	2 ♡	pass
2 ♠ (1)	pass	3 ♣ (2)	pass
3 ♡	pass	4 ♡	pass
pass	pass		

Final contract – Four Hearts

(1) South is not far short of a direct game bid. However, the hand might play better in notrumps, so he chooses to make a trial bid in spades.

(2) North replies with another exploratory bid. The sense of three clubs is, 'I have an honour in clubs but not a strong enough holding to bid 3NT.'

The lead

West leads the jack of clubs. Not wanting to risk a switch to diamonds, which might lead to a ruff, South goes up with the ace of clubs. The queen of hearts hold the next trick. On the jack of hearts East completes a peter in clubs and West holds up again. How should South continue?

Preliminary analysis

As West still has A x of hearts it would be dangerous to play another trump: West would win and play a forcing game in clubs. On the other hand, if trumps are not drawn there is a risk of a diamond ruff. What line gives the best chance?

It cannot be right to continue trumps. West will win and force with a club. Declarer can ruff and draw the last trump, but when he loses to the ace of diamonds he will be defenceless against further club leads.

South may decide, then, to switch to diamonds, hoping that the opponents will not find their ruff. That will fail, against good defence, when the hand is like this:

$$
\begin{array}{c}
\spadesuit \text{ K 10 4} \\
\heartsuit \text{ Q J 9} \\
\diamondsuit \text{ K J 10 8 3} \\
\clubsuit \text{ A 6}
\end{array}
$$

♠ 9 7 2	♠ Q 8 6 3
♡ A 5 4 2	♡ 6
◇ A 2	◇ 7 6 5
♣ K J 10 3	♣ Q 8 7 4 2

$$
\begin{array}{c}
\spadesuit \text{ A J 5} \\
\heartsuit \text{ K 10 8 7 3} \\
\diamondsuit \text{ Q 9 4} \\
\clubsuit \text{ 9 5}
\end{array}
$$

After a club lead and two rounds of hearts declarer leads a diamond. West wins and returns a diamond, and when he comes in with the ace of hearts he will underlead his king of clubs and obtain a ruff.

This sequence could have been averted, as the cards lie, by ducking the first club, but South had his reasons and it is not too late to recover.

After two rounds of hearts South should play a club himself. If West has x x of diamonds a diamond ruff will be unavoidable, assuming good defence, but when West has ◇ A x, as above, the second round of clubs destroys the communications between the defending hands.

Dealer, South   Love all

♠ K 9 4
♡ A 8 5 3
♢ Q 8 4
♣ 9 7 2

♣ Q led

♠ A Q 7 6 5
♡ 7 4
♢ A K 6 3
♣ A 5

The bidding

South	West	North	East
1 ♠	pass	1 NT	pass
2 ♢	pass	3 ♠ (1)	pass
4 ♠	pass	pass	pass

Final contract – Four Spades

(1) The jump preference, following 1NT, is unusual but seems correct here, as North's high cards must all be working well.

The lead

West leads the queen of clubs and East plays the 6. How should South plan the play?

Preliminary analysis

The contract looks promising, but if spades were 4–1 and diamonds 4–2 there might be a loser in each suit. Declarer must direct his mind to that possibility.

Having no premonition of disaster, South won the club lead and played off king and ace of spades. On the second spade West discarded a club, the full hand being:

```
                    ♠ K 9 4
                    ♡ A 8 5 3
                    ◇ Q 8 4
                    ♣ 9 7 2
    ♠ 2                             ♠ J 10 8 3
    ♡ K 9 2                         ♡ Q J 10 6
    ◇ J 9 7 5                       ◇ 10 2
    ♣ Q J 10 8 4                    ♣ K 6 3
                    ♠ A Q 7 6 5
                    ♡ 7 4
                    ◇ A K 6 3
                    ♣ A 5
```

When he found that the spades were not breaking, South turned to the diamonds. To guard against a doubleton diamond with East, he played the ace and crossed to the queen to lead the third diamond from dummy. If East ruffed, he would be ruffing a loser.

However, East did ruff the third diamond and underled his king of clubs to put West in. Another diamond gave East another ruff, and there was still a heart to lose.

South could have avoided this outcome by following general principles at trick one. To restrict communication between the defending hands, he should duck the first club. When East ruffs for the first time he cannot give his partner the lead and the last trump can be drawn.

Note, also, that if West switches to a heart at trick two South must duck this as well. Otherwise, West will have an entry in hearts.

Dealer, North   Love all

♠ 8 6
♡ 10
◇ A K Q 8
♣ A K 10 9 7 5

♡ 4 led

♠ A Q J 3
♡ A J 9 5
◇ 7 6 2
♣ Q 6

The bidding

South	West	North	East
—	—	1 ♣	pass
1 ♡	pass	2 ◇	pass
2 ♠ (1)	pass	3 ♣	pass
3NT	pass	4NT(2)	pass
6NT	pass	pass	pass

Final contract – 6NT

(1) With two aces and the queen of his partner's main suit, South is too strong for 3NT, which could be bid on a weaker hand after his partner's reverse.

(2) Recognizing that his partner has followed a moderately strong sequence, North makes one try. As no suit has been agreed, 4NT is natural.

The lead

West makes the attacking lead of a heart into declarer's bid suit. East plays the queen and South wins with the ace. How should be continue?

Preliminary analysis

If the clubs are breaking, South can count six clubs, three diamonds, one spade, and two hearts after he has given up a trick to the king. However, there may be an entry problem. South must also consider whether he will have any chance if the clubs do not provide six tricks.

Twelve tricks are guaranteed if the clubs break, but South may perceive in time that if he begins with queen and another club he will not be able to develop his second trick in hearts. He may, therefore, have the bright idea of returning the 9 of hearts at trick two.

There is one snag about this: what does he discard from the table? He can throw a spade or a diamond from dummy and still make twelve tricks if the clubs go well, but suppose they do not. In that case he may need the long diamond or a second spade, and probably both. (He cannot, of course, cheerfully discard a club on the second heart, because he is hoping that this suit will provide six tricks.)

The way to escape from this dilemma is to test the clubs without giving up up the entry to hand. In other words, begin with a club to the king and play one back to the queen. That wins the slam when the distribution is:

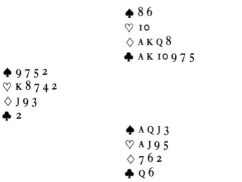

Having won the first trick with the ace of hearts, South plays a club to the king and a club back. Finding that the clubs do not break, he leads the 9 of hearts and discards a club from dummy. As the spade finesse is right and the diamonds break, he makes twelve tricks by way of three spades, two hearts, four diamonds and three clubs. (If the diamonds were not breaking there would be several squeeze chances.)

Dealer, South   *E–W vulnerable*

♠ A 9 8 6 4 3 2
♡ 7 5
◇ Q J 8
♣ 4

♡ J led

♠ 5
♡ A 4
◇ A K 10 9 7 2
♣ K 8 5 3

The bidding

South	West	North	East
1 ◇	2 ◇ (1)	2 ♠	pass
3 ◇	3 ♡	4 ◇	4 ♡
pass	pass	5 ◇ (2)	pass
pass	pass		

Final contract – Five Diamonds

(1) Described as the old-fashioned type of overcall – strong hand with shortage in diamonds.

(2) There may be chances to beat four hearts, but North follows the safer course, in a competitive auction, of bidding one more.

The lead

West leads the jack of hearts and East plays the queen. How should South plan the play?

Preliminary analysis

South has only eight tricks on top. The rest will have to come either from the spade suit or from ruffs in dummy. Which line offers the better prospects?

If there had been no adverse bidding it would be natural to play on the spade suit. With three trump entries to dummy, South can stand a 4–1 break in spades, so long as trumps are not worse than 3–1.

However, it is highly probable, from West's two diamond overcall and subsequent entry into the bidding at the three level, that trumps will be 4–0. If so, the only hope for the contract lies in obtaining three ruffs in dummy.

```
                    ♠ A 9 8 6 4 3 2
                    ♡ 7 5
                    ◇ Q J 8
                    ♣ 4
 ♠ K Q J 7                              ♠ 10
 ♡ K J 10 8 2                           ♡ Q 9 6 3
 ◇ —                                    ◇ 6 5 4 3
 ♣ A Q J 2                              ♣ 10 9 7 6
                    ♠ 5
                    ♡ A 4
                    ◇ A K 10 9 7 2
                    ♣ K 8 5 3
```

South would like to duck the first trick, but East has overtaken the jack of hearts with the queen and threatens to lead a trump. South wins with the ace of hearts, therefore, plays a spade to the ace and returns a spade, intending to discard his second heart whether East ruffs or not. (East, in practice, discards a heart; it would not help him to ruff and lead a trump, as then South would get the spades going.)

West wins the second spade, therefore, while South discards a heart. West exits with a heart and South ruffs. Now he makes the second key play – the king of clubs. West has to win and from this point cannot prevent the declarer from taking three ruffs on the table.

Dealer, South   *Game all*

      ♠ Q 10 8 6
      ♡ 7 4
      ◇ 10 8 6 2
      ♣ Q 10 7

◇ Q led

      ♠ A K 9 7 4
      ♡ A 8
      ◇ A 9 5 3
      ♣ A J

The bidding

South	West	North	East
2 ♣ (1)	pass	2 ◇	pass
2 ♠	pass	4 ♠ (2)	pass
pass	pass		

Final contract – Four Spades

(1) This hand will not necessarily make game opposite a very weak dummy, but that is not the only test that should be applied. Hands with four aces are very powerful opposite any hand that contains a long suit.

(2) This double raise, following a negative, traditionally indicates fair trump support but no first or second round control.

The lead

West leads the queen of diamonds, East plays low and South wins with the ace. Declarer plays off ace and king of spades, West discarding a club on the second round. How should South continue?

Preliminary analysis

South can afford to lose two diamonds and a heart. Alternatively, he may plan to give up a club and discard a heart on dummy's third club. He must consider whether he can afford to draw a third trump and how best to tackle the clubs.

The declarer's first idea was to draw the outstanding trump, then play ace and jack of clubs. The objection to this is that the only entry to dummy will be a fourth spade. When in with the king of clubs the defenders will force out the ace of hearts, and after crossing to dummy South will be out of trumps before he has established his long diamond.

Having reached this conclusion, South played off ace and another club. Now disaster struck from an unexpected angle.

```
                    ♠ Q 10 8 6
                    ♡ 7 4
                    ◊ 10 8 6 2
                    ♣ Q 10 7
  ♠ 5                                    ♠ J 3 2
  ♡ Q 9 2                                ♡ K J 10 6 5 3
  ◊ Q J 4                                ◊ K 7
  ♣ K 9 8 6 4 3                          ♣ 5 2
                    ♠ A K 9 7 4
                    ♡ A 8
                    ◊ A 9 5 3
                    ♣ A J
```

After a diamond to the ace and two top spades declarer sought to clear his club trick by playing ace and jack. But alas, West led a third club, which his partner ruffed with the jack of spades. South disposed of his losing heart on this trick but still had to lose two diamonds.

A slight change in the order of play wins the contract. Instead of playing ace and jack of clubs, South should lead the jack from hand. West wins but cannot stop South from later playing off the ace of clubs and crossing to dummy for a discard on the queen.

Dealer, East   *Love all*

♠ K Q 4
♡ 10 9 6 4
◇ K Q 9
♣ 10 4 2

♣ 3 led

♠ A 5 3
♡ K 5
◇ A 10 8 7 6 5
♣ 8 7

The bidding

South	West	North	East
—	—	—	1 ♣
1 ◇	pass	2 ◇	2 ♠
3 ◇	pass	pass	3 ♠
pass	4 ♣	4 ◇ (1)	pass
pass	pass		

Final contract – Four Diamonds

(1) North's spade holding, after West's preference for clubs, is unfavourable for defence, and while he is prepared to go one down in four diamonds his trumps are fairly good and he does not expect to be doubled.

The lead

West leads a low club. East plays off ace, king and queen of clubs, South ruffing the third round. Declarer plays a low diamond to the king, on which East discards a spade. How should South continue?

Preliminary analysis

On the surface, South has no problem: he can pick up West's J x x x of diamonds and make ten tricks, assuming that East holds the ace of hearts. But is it so easy?

The full hand was:

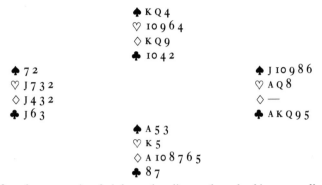

After three rounds of clubs and a diamond to the king, revealing East's void, South returned to the ace of spades and finessed the 9 of diamonds. He realized now that he could not afford to lay down the queen of diamonds and lead a heart, because East would go in with the ace of hearts and play a fourth club. Instead, therefore, he led a heart from the table.

At this point East did well to play low. After South had won with the king of hearts the position was:

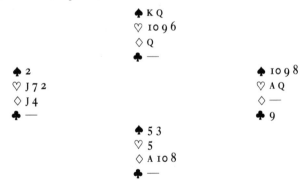

South exited with a heart. East won and played another heart. Now there was no way to escape a trump loser.

South would have been clear of all trouble if he had played a heart instead of a spade from dummy at trick five. The principle is this: when there may be problems in going to and fro, play the slow entry first, keeping the quick entry (the ace of spades) in reserve.

Dealer, South   *Love all*

♠ K 9 4
♡ K 10 8 3
♢ 7 6 5 2
♣ 10 6

♣ 7 led

♠ A 7 6
♡ A 6
♢ A K 9 8 4
♣ A 3 2

The bidding

South	West	North	East
1 ♢	pass	1 ♡	pass
1 ♠ (1)	pass	2 ♢	pass
3NT	pass	pass	pass

Final contract – 3NT

(1) Better than a leap to 3NT. South can cope with a raise in spades, and if partner passes one spade there may be no game in the hand.

The lead
The 7 of clubs is led, East plays the king, and South ducks. East follows with the jack and South plays low again. Declarer wins the next club, discarding a diamond from dummy. How should South continue?

Preliminary analysis
There are seven tricks in aces and kings, and two long diamonds will be enough for game. However, there are still two clubs out and these represent a danger.

This hand is a fairly routine exercise in avoidance play. No doubt West has the remaining clubs, and South must aim to develop the diamonds without letting him into the lead.

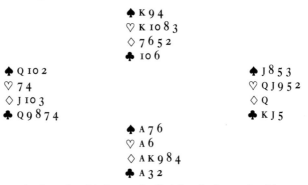

After winning the third round of clubs declarer should cross to dummy and lead a diamond from the table. When the queen appears from East, South ducks, and thereafter he has no problems.

A more subtle example of this form of avoidance play occurred in a par contest (an event with prepared hands) when the critical suit was distributed like this:

```
        A K 9 6 4 2
J                        10 8 5 3
        Q 7
```

South needs five tricks from this suit for game but cannot afford to lose the lead to East. He should begin with a low card from hand. When West, perforce, plays the jack he is allowed to hold the trick.

Dealer, West · *N–S vulnerable*

♠ Q 3
♡ A 6
◇ 8 7 4
♣ A Q 9 8 6 3

♠ 10 led

♠ K 9 6 4
♡ J 10 8 3
◇ K J 10
♣ K J

The bidding

South	West	North	East
—	pass	1 ♣	1 ♠
2NT	3 ♡	3NT (1)	pass
pass	pass		

Final contract – 3NT

(1) The alternative was to pass, giving partner a chance to double three hearts; but North, playing in a pairs, was determined not to be talked out of a vulnerable game that was likely to be bid at other tables.

The lead

West leads the 10 of spades. How should South plan the play?

Preliminary analysis

Barring a 5–0 break, or some difficulty with entries, the clubs should produce six tricks and it is not difficult to find three more. South should consider, therefore, what might go wrong.

The simplest way to develop a ninth trick is to cover the 10 of spades with the queen, preparing for a finesse against the jack. But there may be a snag in that, as South discovered at the table.

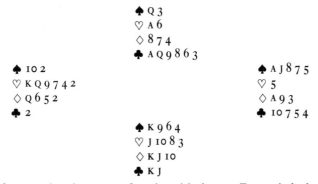

After covering the queen of spades with the ace, East switched to a heart, forcing out dummy's side entry. South finessed the 9 of spades and cashed the king, but his visions of running six club tricks disappeared when West showed out on the second round. In the end he was quite pleased to land eight tricks.

That the clubs would break 4–1 was not at all unlikely in view of the bidding, and South should have forestalled the attack on dummy's entries by playing a low spade from the table at trick one. It would not help East to go up with the ace of spades and attack hearts, so he plays low and the king wins. South plays K J of clubs, leads a heart to the ace, and runs the rest of the clubs. As West did not open the bidding and East has shown nothing but A J x x of spades, South can discard hearts on dummy's clubs and play East for the ace of diamonds.

Dealer, South   Love all

♠ J 9 7 6
♡ 8 4 3
◇ A K 8 5
♣ 10 3

♣ 5 led

♠ 3 2
♡ A K J 10 6 5
◇ 10 4
♣ A Q 8

The bidding

South	West	North	East
1 ♡	pass	1 ♠	pass
3 ♡ (1)	pass	4 ♡	pass
pass	pass		

Final contract – Four Hearts

(1) With about six-and-a-half playing tricks, South is just worth a jump rebid.

The lead

West leads the 5 of clubs, East plays the king and South the ace. As the contract will present no problem if trumps are 2–2 or 3–1, declarer lays down the ace of hearts, on which East discards a diamond. How should South continue?

Preliminary analysis

Unless West has led from a doubleton club (unlikely because in that case East's first discard would have been a club), South can safely ruff the third round of clubs. After that, his only concern will be not to lose two trump tricks.

At the table South blithely continued with queen of clubs, club ruff, heart to the king and jack of hearts, taken by West's queen. West exited with a diamond and for the first time declarer began to have forebodings.

```
                    ♠ J 9 7 6
                    ♡ 8 4 3
                    ◇ A K 8 5
                    ♣ 10 3
  ♠ A K 10                              ♠ Q 8 5 4
  ♡ Q 9 7 2                             ♡ –
  ◇ 9 2                                 ◇ Q J 7 6 3
  ♣ J 7 6 5                             ♣ K 9 4 2
                    ♠ 3 2
                    ♡ A K J 10 6 5
                    ◇ 10 4
                    ♣ A Q 8
```

The play so far has been: club to king and ace, ace of hearts, queen of clubs and club ruff, king and jack of hearts, won by West, diamond to the king.

Anxious now about entries to his own hand, South played a low spade from the table. Hot on the trail, West won with the king and led his second diamond. When South led another spade from the table East went up with the queen and led a diamond, promoting his partner's 9 of hearts.

It was a well played defence, but South could have averted the trump promotion by playing a spade at an early stage. Say that the defenders exit with a diamond. South plays another spade, and the difference is that when West later comes in with the queen of hearts he cannot give his partner the lead to play a third diamond.

Dealer, South   *Love all*

           ♠ K 10 8
           ♡ J 8 6 5 4
           ◇ 6
           ♣ A K J 5

♣ 10 led

           ♠ A
           ♡ K Q 10 9 7
           ◇ A K Q J 4
           ♣ 6 2

The bidding

South	West	North	East
1 ♡	pass	2 ♣ (1)	pass
3 ◇	pass	3 ♡ (2)	pass
3 ♠	pass	4NT	pass
5 ♡	pass	6 ♡	pass
pass	pass		

Final contract – Six Hearts

(1) Too strong for a direct raise to four, North plans the stronger sequence of a change of suit, to be followed by a jump to game.

(2) Now a jump to four hearts would be limited and quite inadequate.

The lead
West leads the 10 of clubs and dummy's ace wins. How should South plan the play?

Preliminary analysis
The contract looks safe, with just the ace of hearts to lose. This is the time to consider, what could go wrong?

The only possible danger lies in a club ruff, and the best protection against this is to eliminate the clubs from one hand or the other. It may be possible to discard dummy's clubs on the declarer's diamonds, but a safer plan is to dispose of declarer's second club.

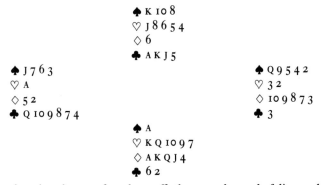

South cashes the ace of spades, ruffs the second round of diamonds, and discards a club on the king of spades. Then it is safe to play trumps.

Dealer, East   Love all

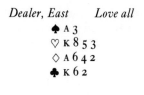

♠ A 3
♡ K 8 5 3
◇ A 6 4 2
♣ K 6 2

◇ J led

♠ K Q 10 9 7 6 5
♡ 6 2
◇ 3
♣ A 7 3

The bidding

South	West	North	East
—	—	—	1 ◇
2 ♠ (1)	pass	4 ♠	pass
pass	pass		

Final contract – Four Spades

(1) An intermediate jump overcall, suggesting the values for an opening bid with a good six-card or longer suit.

The lead
West leads the jack of diamonds. Declarer goes up with the ace and East drops the 8. How should South plan the play?

Preliminary analysis
If the spades break, or if West shows out when the ace is led, South cannot fail to make ten tricks. He must address his mind, therefore, to the possibility that the spades will be awkward. In that case, where can he go for a tenth trick?

To play the ace of spades at trick two seems natural enough, but it gives away the contract when the cards lie in this fashion:

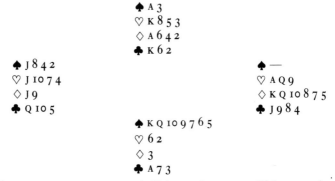

```
                        ♠ A 3
                        ♡ K 8 5 3
                        ◇ A 6 4 2
                        ♣ K 6 2
    ♠ J 8 4 2                              ♠ —
    ♡ J 10 7 4                             ♡ A Q 9
    ◇ J 9                                  ◇ K Q 10 8 7 5
    ♣ Q 10 5                               ♣ J 9 8 4
                        ♠ K Q 10 9 7 6 5
                        ♡ 6 2
                        ◇ 3
                        ♣ A 7 3
```

The contract can go wrong only if the spades are 4–0. If they are, the best chance for a tenth trick is to bring down the ace of hearts in three rounds. South will need to ruff the third round and to get back to dummy to make the king; to do this, he must keep the ace of spades as an entry card.

The right play at trick two is a low heart from the table. East wins and plays a high diamond, which South ruffs. Now the king of spades should be led, for if spades are 3–1 declarer can simply cross to the ace and return with a club to draw the last trump.

As it happens, East shows out on the king of spades. South plays a second heart, ducking in dummy. If West takes this trick he can do no damage, and if East wins with the 9 and plays another diamond South simply ruffs with the 10. West makes his trump trick, but with the ace of spades and king of clubs still in dummy South can make a trick with the king of hearts.

Note that it is not good enough to cross to the king of spades at trick two and lead a heart. West goes in with the 10 of hearts and if allowed to hold the trick plays a second trump. This takes an entry out of dummy before South is ready to ruff hearts.

Dealer, West   *Love all*

          ♠ A Q 9 8 7 4
          ♡ 9 8 7 5 3
          ◊ 7 4
          ♣ —

♣ K led

          ♠ K J 10 3
          ♡ A K 4
          ◊ K 9 3
          ♣ J 6 5

The bidding

South	West	North	East
—	1 ◊	2 ◊ (1)	pass
3 ♠	4 ♣	4 ♠	5 ♣
pass (2)	pass	5 ♠	pass
pass	pass		

Final contract – Five Spades

(1) This is the Michaels cue-bid, showing a moderate hand with length in both majors.

(2) Correctly leaving the decision to partner, because despite his 15 points South has only moderate defence against a club contract.

The lead

West leads the king of clubs and dummy ruffs. How should South plan the play?

Preliminary analysis

West appears to have ten or eleven cards in the minor suits, including, no doubt, the ace of diamonds. Thus South is in danger of losing a heart and two diamonds. If he plays on reverse dummy lines, ruffing three clubs on the table, his total of winners is only nine – four trumps in hand, three ruffs, and two hearts.

South may spend time looking for ways to make the contract against a 4–1 break in hearts, but it can't be done. He may force West to open up the diamonds or concede a ruff-and-discard, but he will not be able to get a fifth heart going as well.

To make the contract, South must find the hearts 3–2 and must prevent East from gaining the lead.

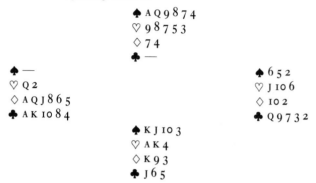

After ruffing the first club in dummy, South leads the 7 of hearts. If East puts in the jack South wins with the ace, draws trumps, and leads another heart from dummy. If East plays low on the first heart, so does South.

Note that, as the cards lie, South can be defeated if he comes to hand with a trump and leads the ace of hearts. West must unblock and then East cannot be kept out of the lead.

Dealer, West   *Love all*

        ♠ K Q 8
        ♡ Q 3
        ◊ Q J 9 7 3 2
        ♣ A K

♡ K led

        ♠ A J 10 4
        ♡ 10 7 5 2
        ◊ A 5
        ♣ 8 3 2

The bidding

South	West	North	East
—	1 ♡	dble	pass
2 ♠	pass	3 ♠ (1)	pass
4 ♠	pass	pass	pass

Final contract – Four Spades

(1) North's spades are not good for this sequence, but there seems to be little point in introducing his diamond suit.

The lead

On West's lead of the king of hearts East drops the jack. West continues with ace of hearts, on which East discards a club, and a third heart. South ruffs with the queen of spades in dummy and East throws another club. South draws four rounds of trumps, West discarding one heart and one club. How should South play now?

Preliminary analysis

South has so far lost two tricks and made five. The 10 of hearts is good, he has three top winners in the minor suits, and it should be possible to establish a further trick in diamonds. But what is the safest way to organize this?

These are the remaining cards:

♠ —
♡ —
◊ Q J 9 7
♣ A K

♠ —
♡ 10
◊ A 5
♣ 8 3 2

South has an entry problem. If he cashes the 10 of hearts and then plays ace and another diamond, there is an obvious danger that West may make the king of diamonds and his remaining heart. The objection to crossing to dummy and taking a diamond finesse is that if it loses, and a club comes back, the remaining diamonds will be blocked.

South decided at the table to play ace and another diamond without cashing the 10 of hearts. This would have been all right against any 3–2 break in diamonds, but the full hand was:

```
                    ♠ K Q 8
                    ♡ Q 3
                    ◊ Q J 9 7 3 2
                    ♣ A K
  ♠ 7 5                              ♠ 9 6 3 2
  ♡ A K 9 8 6 4                      ♡ J
  ◊ 6                                ◊ K 10 8 4
  ♣ Q J 9 5                          ♣ 10 7 6 4
                    ♠ A J 10 4
                    ♡ 10 7 5 2
                    ◊ A 5
                    ♣ 8 3 2
```

South lost two diamond tricks at the finish.

In the first diagram there was a safe way to hold everything together: declarer plays a low diamond from hand, not the ace.

This form of play is often overlooked. At notrumps, for example, after the ace of a suit has gone, declarer holds K x opposite J 10 x or J 10 x x. For reasons of entry and control, the best play may be to lead low from hand.

Dealer, South   *Love all*

           ♠ A 10 7
           ♡ J 4 2
           ◇ K 8
           ♣ K J 9 7 4

♣ 3 led

           ♠ 3
           ♡ A Q
           ◇ J 9 6 5 4 2
           ♣ A Q 10 8

The bidding

South	West	North	East
1 ◇	pass	2NT (1)	pass
3 ♣	pass	3 ♠ (2)	pass
3NT	pass	5 ♣	pass
pass	pass		

Final contract – Five Clubs

(1) Not necessarily recommended, but a bid that many players would make at rubber bridge.

(2) North's hand looks strong when his partner bids clubs. He intends to raise to five clubs at least, and meanwhile he makes an advance cue-bid in spades.

The lead

West leads the 3 of clubs and all follow to two rounds of trumps. How should South plan the play?

Preliminary analysis

South has to avoid the loss of two diamonds and a heart. Assuming that the heart finesse is wrong, for otherwise there is no problem, what is the best way to tackle the diamonds?

Declarer's objective is to get the diamonds going without giving East a chance to take the first diamond and lead a heart through the A Q.

The straightforward play of a diamond to the king will be good enough whenever West holds the ace but will fail (assuming the heart finesse to be wrong) when East holds the ace.

Alternatively, South can play West for the queen by leading the jack from his own hand. If West plays the queen he is allowed to hold the trick and cannot effectively attack hearts.

So far, then, South can play West for the ace or for the queen, both even chances. There is one line of play that will improve the odds. Assume the distribution to be:

```
                  ♠ A 10 7
                  ♡ J 4 2
                  ◇ K 8
                  ♣ K J 9 7 4
♠ J 9 8 4 2                        ♠ K Q 6 5
♡ K 6 5 3                          ♡ 10 9 8 7
◇ A 3                             ◇ Q 10 7
♣ 5 3                             ♣ 6 2
                  ♠ 3
                  ♡ A Q
                  ◇ J 9 6 5 4 2
                  ♣ A Q 10 8
```

South wins the second trump in dummy and leads a low diamond from the table. This always wins when West has the queen, because South will have time to get the diamonds going for a heart discard. The chances are the same as the play mentioned above – leading the jack of diamonds from hand. But there is the substantial extra chance that East, holding Q x or Q x x, will fail to go up with the queen in second position. He should do, certainly, but many players wouldn't, and for that reason the low diamond is the best psychological play. It happens to be the wrong method as the cards lie above, but it may still succeed.

Dealer, North   Love all

♠ J 7 6 2
♡ 10 5 4 3
◇ A
♣ A Q 7 3

◇ 5 led

♠ A 8
♡ A K Q 9 6 2
◇ K 6 2
♣ 8 5

The bidding

South	West	North	East
—	—	1 ♣	pass
2 ♡	pass	3 ♡	pass
3 ♠	pass	4 ◇ (1)	pass
4NT	pass	5 ♡	pass
5NT (2)	pass	6 ♣	pass
6 ♡	pass	pass	pass

Final contract – Six Hearts

(1) Although he has opened on such a minimum hand, North is not wrong to show a control below game level.

(2) If his partner will admit to possession of two kings, South will try for a grand slam.

The lead

West leads the 5 of diamonds to dummy's ace, East playing the 8. How should South plan the play?

Preliminary analysis

South is one trick short and the contract appears to depend on the club finesse. Is there any way of improving on this?

Declarer can give himself a slight extra chance by playing off ace and another spade before taking the club finesse. If he finds East with K Q x, for example, he can ruff out the third round. But this is a slender hope and there is something better.

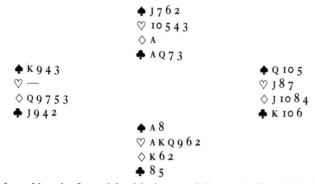

After taking the first trick with the ace of diamonds, South led a low club from the table. From East's point of view, South might have held J x of clubs, and it flashed through his mind that it might be good defence to go up with the king and attempt to force the table with a diamond; but it didn't flash quickly enough, for though he played a low club he gave away the position of the king. West returned a club immediately, but South went up with the ace and ruffed the next round.

This simple manoeuvre of leading low from the A Q, when the finesse can be taken later, is always worth trying. A defender with K 10 x x will sometimes go up with the king for fear that the declarer is playing up to J x.

Dealer, *West*   Love all

♠ A K Q 4
♡ 10 4 3
◇ Q 8 6 4 3
♣ Q

♡ K led

♠ 9 7 6 5 3
♡ Q 2
◇ K 5
♣ A 10 7 2

The bidding

South	West	North	East
—	pass	1 ◇	pass
1 ♠	pass	2 ♠	pass
3 ♣ (1)	pass	4 ♠	pass
pass	pass		

Final contract – Four Spades

(1) South is just about worth a game try.

The lead

West leads the king of hearts and follows with ace and jack, which South ruffs. East follows suit with the 6, 7 and 8. How should South plan the play?

Preliminary analysis

South cannot ruff all his club losers without establishing a trump trick for the opposition, so he must aim to develop at least one long card in diamonds. The problem is how best to establish the diamonds without running short of entries or sustaining a ruff.

Clearly it would not be good play to draw trumps before tackling the diamonds, as dummy would be short of entries unless both suits broke well. Appreciating this, the declarer led the king of diamonds from hand. When this was allowed to hold, he played another diamond, ducking in dummy. This proved unavailing, for the full hand was:

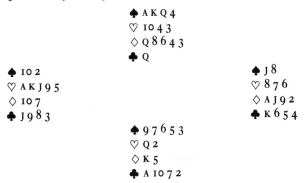

♠ A K Q 4
♡ 10 4 3
◊ Q 8 6 4 3
♣ Q

♠ 10 2
♡ A K J 9 5
◊ 10 7
♣ J 9 8 3

♠ J 8
♡ 8 7 6
◊ A J 9 2
♣ K 6 5 4

♠ 9 7 6 5 3
♡ Q 2
◊ K 5
♣ A 10 7 2

East won the second diamond with the jack and took the only chance by leading a third diamond, for his partner to ruff.

It would not have helped declarer, after the king of diamonds had held, to draw trumps, as he would have been short of entries to cash a long diamond.

The contract cannot be made against best defence, but South could have set a neat trap. East is marked with the ace of diamonds, as West passed originally and has turned up with good hearts. Declarer must try and persuade East to take his ace of diamonds on the first round. The best chance was to lead a low diamond to the queen. It would take a good player to hold off this lead; if East wins and plays a trump, South can return to the king of diamonds, draw a second trump and eventually enjoy the fifth diamond.

Dealer, North   *N–S vulnerable*

♠ J 5 3
♡ A K 9 8 4
◇ A J 5
♣ J 7

♠ 6 led

♠ A Q 4
♡ 10 2
◇ K Q 10 6
♣ 8 6 4 2

The bidding

South	West	North	East
—	—	1 ♡	1 ♠
2NT	3 ♣	3NT (1)	pass
pass	pass		

Final contract – 3NT

(1) Playing in a pairs event, North tries for a vulnerable game rather than take a penalty from three clubs.

The lead
West leads the 6 of spades, dummy plays low and East puts on the 7. How should South plan the play?

Preliminary analysis
There are only eight tricks on top and the ninth must presumably come from hearts. However, there is not much chance of a double finesse against the Q J succeeding, and as soon as the opponents come in they will run off several tricks in clubs. Is there any way to prevent this?

Before playing to the first trick, South should consider what the club distribution is likely to be. West has come in with three clubs and must have six, but as he did not lead a club they canot be headed by the A K Q. The odds are that East has a singleton king, or conceivably a singleton queen.

Once he has reached this conclusion, South may see a way to put West under pressure. The hand may well be like this:

```
                      ♠ J 5 3
                      ♡ A K 9 8 4
                      ◇ A J 5
                      ♣ J 7
      ♠ 6 2                              ♠ K 10 9 8 7
      ♡ J 6                              ♡ Q 7 5 3
      ◇ 9 4 2                            ◇ 8 7 3
      ♣ A Q 10 9 5 3                     ♣ K
                      ♠ A Q 4
                      ♡ 10 2
                      ◇ K Q 10 6
                      ♣ 8 6 4 2
```

South wins the first spade with the queen and leads a low club, straight into enemy-held territory. Now, to beat the hand, West must play the crocodile coup, opening his jaws wide to swallow his partner's king. There is a good chance, however, that West will think that declarer, holding the king of clubs, is trying to sneak a ninth trick. If he thinks this – or doesn't think at all – West will play the queen and the club suit will be dead. East cannot play spades and declarer will easily establish dummy's hearts, ending up with ten tricks, as the cards lie.

Dealer, South   *Game all*

♠ 7 4
♡ K 8
◇ A Q 9 6 5 4
♣ J 10 6

♠ 3 led

♠ A 10
♡ Q 9 6 3
◇ K 8
♣ A 9 8 5 2

The bidding

South	West	North	East
1 ♣	pass	1 ◇	pass
1NT (1)	pass	3NT (2)	pass
pass	pass		

Final contract – 3NT

(1) A rebid of one heart would be more orthodox, but South chooses to make the limited bid that expresses his range.

(2) North is slightly short in points for this raise, but such contracts usually depend on whether the diamond suit can be brought in. Often it is a question of nine tricks or seven.

The lead

West leads the 3 of spades and East plays the queen. How should South plan the play?

Preliminary analysis

Both hands, unfortunately, are short in spades, so as soon as the opponents come in they will be able to take at least four spades and a heart. Is there any way to confuse or deflect them?

First, it is correct to take the queen of spades with the ace; to hold up will make it easy for both defenders to judge the spade situation.

The hand proved interesting in a team event because the two declarers tried different ruses in an attempt to snatch a heart trick before the opponents could tell what was happening. The first declarer tried a manoeuvre that was credited to Josephine Culbertson forty years ago: he laid down the king of diamonds, then played a heart towards the table. The idea was that if West held a doubleton diamond he might conclude that his partner held the suit and that there was no urgency to take the ace of hearts immediately. With modern signalling methods, it wasn't difficult for the defenders to avoid this trap.

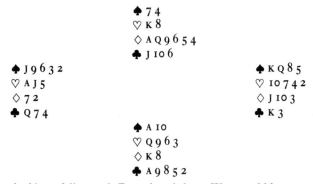

On the king of diamonds East played the 3. West could be sure that with four diamonds his partner would have signalled with the 8, so when the low heart followed he hopped up with the ace and led another spade.

At the other table South made a shrewder play. At trick two he laid down the ace of clubs, gravely unblocking with dummy's 10. When the ace of clubs was followed by a low heart West, convinced that declarer was intending to play on the club suit, was lulled into playing low. South then hastily took his six diamond tricks.

Dealer, South   *Love all*

           ♠ A 9 7 5
           ♡ K J 8 4
           ◊ Q 10 2
           ♣ J 6

◊ 9 led

           ♠ K 10 8 4
           ♡ —
           ◊ A 6
           ♣ A K Q 8 7 5 2

The bidding

South	West	North	East
1 ♣	pass	1 ♡	pass
1 ♠ (1)	pass	3 ♠	pass
6 ♠ (2)	pass	pass	pass

Final contract – Six Spades

(1) The most economical way to develop the hand: a jump in clubs can come later.

(2) After the unexpected double raise, a slam is likely. By playing in spades, presumably a 4–4 fit, South hopes to escape a diamond loser, as it should be possible to discard dummy's diamonds on the long clubs.

The lead

West leads the 9 of diamonds. South puts in the 10 from dummy and this is covered by the jack and ace. All play low on the king of spades. How should South continue?

Preliminary analysis

South sees that it was right to play in spades rather than clubs, but the diamond lead is unfortunate for him. He must assume that the spades are 3–2, and if the hand with three trumps also holds three clubs it will be possible to discard dummy's diamonds in time. But supposing the distribution is not so favourable, is there anything he can do to improve his chances?

South plays a second round of spades to the ace, and all follow, East dropping the jack. Now a low heart from the table might conceivably trap East into playing the ace, but if East is a fair player he will recall that South leaped into the slam without using Blackwood and is likely therefore to hold a void.

A better idea is to play the clubs in a deceptive order that may lead West (assuming he holds the missing trump) to believe that the suit is not solid. Suppose that the hand is like this:

```
                    ♠ A 9 7 5
                    ♡ K J 8 4
                    ◇ Q 10 2
                    ♣ J 6
 ♠ Q 6 3                                 ♠ J 2
 ♡ Q 10 7 5                              ♡ A 9 6 3 2
 ◇ 9 8 7 4                               ◇ K J 5 3
 ♣ 9 3                                   ♣ 10 4
                    ♠ K 10 8 4
                    ♡ —
                    ◇ A 6
                    ♣ A K Q 8 7 5 2
```

After two rounds of spades declarer leads a club to the queen, cashes the ace, and follows with a low one. Now, unless West is a very thoughtful player who will consider the implications of the bidding, he will assume that his partner still holds the king of clubs and that South is intending to ruff in dummy. He may well fail to go in with the queen of spades and play a second diamond. If West does not ruff, South discards a diamond from the table and continues clubs.

Another setting for this type of play occurs when a side suit is distributed like this:

```
            K J 10 4
 9 7 3 2                        8 5
            A Q 6
```

Hoping to discard a loser from his own hand, declarer plays the ace, then low to the king, and the jack from dummy. If East fails to ruff, South will return to dummy for a discard on the 10.

Dealer, South   Love all

            ♠ K J 10 5
            ♡ K J 4
            ◇ 8 7 3
            ♣ K 6 2

♣ Q led

            ♠ Q
            ♡ A Q 10 8 5 2
            ◇ J 10 5 2
            ♣ A 7

The bidding

South	West	North	East
1 ♡	pass	1 ♠	pass
2 ♡	pass	3 ♡ (1)	pass
4 ♡	pass	pass	pass

Final contract – Four Hearts

(1) A bid of 2NT at this point might have led to a better contract, but the raise in hearts was not unreasonable.

The lead
West leads the queen of clubs and East plays the 5. How should South plan the play?

Preliminary analysis
South is threatened with the loss of three diamonds and a spade. It is possible that when they take their spade trick the opponents will not be able to run three tricks in diamonds. Has South any other chance?

The straightforward line is to win with the ace of clubs, draw trumps, and lead the 10 of spades from the table. This might put East under some pressure if he held the ace. Even if the opponents take their spade trick, South will still succeed if either defender has a singleton honour in diamonds or two honours alone.

That is a fairly slender chance, and there is a deceptive play that will win almost half the time.

```
                    ♠ K J 10 5
                    ♡ K J 4
                    ◇ 8 7 3
                    ♣ K 6 2
♠ 9 7 4 3 2                            ♠ A 8 6
♡ 7                                    ♡ 9 6 3
◇ A 9 4                                ◇ K Q 6
♣ Q J 10 4                            ♣ 9 8 5 3
                    ♠ Q
                    ♡ A Q 10 8 5 2
                    ◇ J 10 5 2
                    ♣ A 7
```

The queen of clubs is led, and South ducks in both hands! West will surely follow with the jack of clubs. South wins with the ace, plays ace of hearts and a heart to the king, then discards the queen of spades on the king of clubs. Now he takes the ruffing finesse against the ace of spades and re-enters dummy with the jack of hearts to discard two diamonds on the established spades.

This line is almost sure to succeed whenever East holds the ace of spades; and if West holds this card he is bound to switch to diamonds when he comes in, so ducking the first club is unlikely to cost the contract.

Dealer, West   *Love all*

         ♠ 8 7 6 4
         ♡ 6
         ◇ A Q J 9 5
         ♣ 9 7 4

◇ 6 led

         ♠ K Q J 9 2
         ♡ A Q 4
         ◇ K 8
         ♣ J 5 2

The bidding

South	West	North	East
—	1 ♡	pass	pass
dble	pass	2 ◇	pass
2 ♠	pass	4 ♠ (1)	pass
pass	pass		

Final contract – Four Spades

(1) Three-and-a-half spades, anyway!

The lead
West leads the 6 of diamonds. How should South plan the play?

Preliminary analysis
If South leads a spade at once, the defenders are likely to find their club tricks. South might play for a quick discard on the diamonds, but a 3–3 break is unlikely after the diamond lead. Is there anything else he can try?

West would hardly have chosen to lead from three small in a suit bid by dummy, so to play off three rounds of diamonds is a forlorn hope.

Looking for a deceptive play, South might think of going up with the ace of diamonds and playing a spade from the table. But East would play his lowest diamond on the first trick and the club switch would be marked.

Looking at the full diagram, can you see a plan that might well come off?

```
                    ♠ 8 7 6 4
                    ♡ 6
                    ◇ A Q J 9 5
                    ♣ 9 7 4
  ♠ A 10                              ♠ 5 3
  ♡ K 9 8 7 3 2                       ♡ J 10 5
  ◇ 6 2                               ◇ 10 7 4 3
  ♣ A Q 10                            ♣ K 8 6 3
                    ♠ K Q J 9 2
                    ♡ A Q 4
                    ◇ K 8
                    ♣ J 5 2
```

Suppose that South wins the diamond lead with the king and plays the queen of hearts from hand! West may get it into his head that his partner holds the ace and may let the queen pass so that East can play a club through declarer's king. If West falls for this play, a club from dummy can be discarded on the ace of hearts.

Dealer, South   *E–W vulnerable*

♠ A 10 6 4 2
♡ 10 5 3
◇ 4
♣ A 9 7 4

♠ 9 led

♠ K Q J 5 3
♡ Q 8
◇ K Q J 7
♣ 6 3

The bidding

South	West	North	East
1 ♠	dble	4 ♠ (1)	pass
pass	pass		

Final contract – Four Spades

(1) North is strong enough to redouble, but at the score he prefers to make it difficult for the opponents to come in.

The lead
West leads the 9 of spades, East following suit with the 7. How should South plan the play?

Preliminary analysis
The hands fit badly, with duplication of values in diamonds. Even after the ace of diamonds has been forced out, the defence may take two hearts, a diamond and a club. Is there any tactical manoeuvre that will give South a chance to prevent this?

One point that should occur to the declarer is that, if he proposes to play a diamond to one of his honours, he should do this at once, before drawing a second round of trumps.

```
                    ♠ A 10 6 4 2
                    ♡ 10 5 3
                    ◇ 4
                    ♣ A 9 7 4
  ♠ 9 8                              ♠ 7
  ♡ A J 7 4                          ♡ K 9 6 2
  ◇ A 10 9 5                         ◇ 8 6 3 2
  ♣ K J 10                           ♣ Q 8 5 2
                    ♠ K Q J 5 3
                    ♡ Q 8
                    ◇ K Q J 7
                    ♣ 6 3
```

Clearly it would be a mistake to draw a second trump, giving East a chance to signal with the 9 of hearts.

South might try the stratagem of winning the first trick in his own hand and leading the jack of diamonds. It is unlikely, however, that West would be so naive as to play low. When West won with the ace East might drop the 8, a suit-preference signal to show that he would welcome a switch to the higher-valued suit, hearts.

One ingenious plan has a good chance of success. South takes the first trick in dummy, leads the 4 of diamonds and puts in the 7 from hand. West wins with the 9 and may not credit declarer with such strong diamonds. If he continues with a 'safe' trump, declarer can lead the king of diamonds through the ace and obtain two heart discards.

Dealer, West   Love all

♠ A 8 6 4 3
♡ A 5
◇ A 9 7 4
♣ K 7

♡ K led

♠ K Q 10 2
♡ 7 4
◇ —
♣ J 9 6 5 4 3 2

The bidding

South	West	North	East
—	1 ♡	dble	3 ♡
3 ♠ (1)	pass	4 ♠	pass
pass	pass		

Final contract – Four Spades

(1) A rather difficult choice: if clubs, how many? South decides to rely on the general principle that a player who doubles one major must have fair support for the other.

The lead

West leads the king of hearts. The ace wins and East drops the 6. How should South plan the play?

Preliminary analysis

A 4–0 trump break might be awkward, but otherwise the contract does not look too difficult. South has to consider the relative merits of a cross-ruff and of playing to establish the clubs.

The declarer made a muddle of this hand. He hastily discarded a heart on the ace of diamonds, then crossed to the king of spades and led a club to the king and ace.

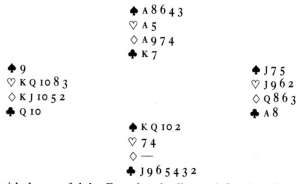

♠ A 8 6 4 3
♡ A 5
◇ A 9 7 4
♣ K 7

♠ 9
♡ K Q 10 8 3
◇ K J 10 5 2
♣ Q 10

♠ J 7 5
♡ J 9 6 2
◇ Q 8 6 3
♣ A 8

♠ K Q 10 2
♡ 7 4
◇ —
♣ J 9 6 5 4 3 2

In with the ace of clubs, East played a diamond, South ruffing. West won the next club and played another diamond, reducing declarer to one trump. When West showed out on the queen of spades South still had to lose a trump and one of the red cards in dummy.

The hand plays quite easily if South does not fall for the trap of taking a discard on the ace of diamonds. He can afford to lose two clubs and one other trick, but must on no account weaken his own hand.

After ace of hearts he plays a spade to the queen and leads a club, losing to East. The defenders cash a heart and play a diamond, won by dummy's ace. A second club is lost and the rest of the hand is straightforward.

Dealer, South   Game all

♠ Q 9 8
♡ 2
◇ A K 9 3
♣ K Q 7 4 2

♠ 3 led

♠ A K J 7
♡ A 10 5 4 3
◇ 7 4
♣ A 3

The bidding

South	West	North	East
1 ♡	pass	2 ♣	pass
2 ♠	pass	2NT (1)	pass
3NT	pass	4 ◇	pass
5 ♣	pass	5 ♠	pass
6 ♠ (2)	pass	pass	pass

Final contract – Six Spades

(1) After a response at the two level and a reverse by opener, 2NT is forcing. North makes a mark-time bid to learn more about partner's hand.

(2) South has not much in reserve, but his trumps are good and he has three aces. If North is not serious about spades he can always revert to notrumps.

The lead

West leads the 3 of spades and dummy's 8 holds the trick, East playing the 2. How should South plan the play?

Preliminary analysis

South has ten top winners and can reasonably count on one ruff in hearts. He may try to ruff two hearts, but there are entry problems. One heart ruff plus four tricks in clubs would be enough, but if spades and clubs are both 4–2 the exact sequence of play will need careful organization.

Declarer should see first that if spades are 4–2 he cannot conveniently ruff two hearts. After ace of hearts and a heart ruff, club to ace and a heart ruff, he can return to hand only by shortening his trumps.

A better line is to take one ruff, draw trumps, then play on clubs. This wins if spades are 3–3 and clubs 4–2, or if spades are 4–2 and clubs 3–3, but is likely to fail when both suits are 4–2, as here:

```
                    ♠ Q 9 8
                    ♡ 2
                    ◇ A K 9 3
                    ♣ K Q 7 4 2
  ♠ 10 6 5 3                        ♠ 4 2
  ♡ K J 9 7                         ♡ Q 8 6
  ◇ 10 5 2                          ◇ Q J 8 6
  ♣ 10 6                            ♣ J 9 8 5
                    ♠ A K J 7
                    ♡ A 10 5 4 3
                    ◇ 7 4
                    ♣ A 3
```

The play goes: spade to 8, ace of hearts and heart ruff, queen of spades, club to ace, draw remaining trumps. Now, when the clubs do not break, East comes in to lead a heart, while declarer has no more trumps.

There is one play, not at all uncommon on hands of this type, that keeps everything under control: South should duck a club at trick two!

Suppose the defenders play back a trump. South takes his heart ruff, comes to hand with ace of clubs, and draws the remaining trumps; then a diamond to the king, and the rest of the clubs are good.

Dealer, North   Love all

♠ A Q 8 6 4
♡ A K 5 4 2
◇ Q 6 3
♣ —

◇ A led

♠ K 7
♡ 10 3
◇ K J 10 9 7 4
♣ K 6 3

The bidding

South	West	North	East
—	—	1 ♠	pass
2 ◇	pass	2 ♡	pass
2NT	pass	3 ◇	pass
4 ◇ (1)	pass	6 ◇ (2)	pass
pass	pass		

Final contract – Six Diamonds

(1) As North is bidding constructively, South takes this opportunity to confirm that his diamonds are a useful suit.

(2) North does not try for a grand slam because his partner can hardly hold sufficiently good diamonds plus a club guard (as indicated by his 2NT rebid) and a high honour in one of the major suits.

The lead

West leads the ace of diamonds and plays a second round, to which all follow. How should South plan the play?

Preliminary analysis

South can count five diamonds in his own hand, one ruff, and four top winners in the major suits. He needs only to establish one long-card winner. West's lead of ace and another trump is perhaps a warning that the suits are not breaking well.

If South plays first on his stronger suit, spades, he loses the contract when the distribution is:

```
              ♠ A Q 8 6 4
              ♡ A K 5 4 2
              ◇ Q 6 3
              ♣ —
♠ J 9 5 3 2                      ♠ 10
♡ 7 6                           ♡ Q J 9 8
◇ A 5                           ◇ 8 2
♣ A Q 9 7                       ♣ J 10 8 5 4 2
              ♠ K 7
              ♡ 10 3
              ◇ K J 10 9 7 4
              ♣ K 6 3
```

After ace and another diamond South plays king and ace of spades. When this suit breaks 5–1 he has no time to establish a long heart. If he were to play on hearts first he would be able to claim the contract after two rounds.

Now suppose that the major suits were the other way round – spades 4–2 and hearts 5–1. Playing on hearts first would not be fatal, because there would still be time to set up a long spade. Thus the usual principle on such occasions is to test the weaker suit first.

Dealer, West   Game all

♠ 6 4
♡ 9 2
◇ K 10 7 4 3
♣ 8 7 5 2

♠ 8 led

♠ A K 5
♡ A K Q J 10
◇ 5
♣ K Q 6 4

The bidding

South	West	North	East
—	pass	pass	1 ♠
dble	pass	2 ◇	pass
3 ♡ (1)	pass	4 ♡ (2)	pass
pass	pass		

Final contract – Four Hearts

(1) South has a fairly close choice between 3NT and a jump in hearts. The 150 honours in hearts perhaps sway the balance.

(2) South's bidding is very strong and North has just enough for the raise.

The lead

West leads the 8 of spades and declarer plays three rounds. West follows suit and dummy ruffs low. South uses the entry to play a club to the king, which holds. How should he continue?

Preliminary analysis

Nine sure tricks are in sight and one further trick from clubs will be enough. What is the safest way to develop this extra trick?

It would not be good play to draw trumps at this point, because if hearts were 4–2 and East had, say, A J x of clubs, declarer would lose control before he could enjoy the fourth round of clubs.

Realizing that the 9 of hearts in dummy would protect him from being forced in spades, South exited with a low club before drawing any trumps. That didn't quite work either, for the full hand was:

```
                    ♠ 6 4
                    ♡ 9 2
                    ◇ K 10 7 4 3
                    ♣ 8 7 5 2
  ♠ 8 7 2                              ♠ Q J 10 9 3
  ♡ 7 6 5 3                            ♡ 8 4
  ◇ Q 9 6 2                            ◇ A J 8
  ♣ J 3                               ♣ A 10 9
                    ♠ A K 5
                    ♡ A K Q J 10
                    ◇ 5
                    ♣ K Q 6 4
```

After three rounds of spades and a club to the king, South returned a low club, won by the jack. West now exited with a diamond. Declarer played the 10 from dummy, but East won with the jack and led the ace. South had to ruff, and after four rounds of trumps East was left with the ace of clubs and a winning spade.

It was a well played defence, but South missed a trick. After the king of clubs he should have exited with the queen, not a low one. With East on lead, he cannot be forced in diamonds and dummy's 9 of hearts will take care of the spades.

Dealer, South   Love all

♠ K Q 3
♡ 6 2
◇ 8 5 3 2
♣ K Q J 4

◇ K led

♠ A J 7 2
♡ A J 10 5
◇ 4
♣ A 10 8 7

The bidding

South	West	North	East
1 ♣	2 ◇	3 ♣	pass
3 ♡	pass	3 ♠	pass
4 ♠ (1)	pass	5 ♣	pass
pass	pass		

Final contract – Five Clubs

(1) South knows that his partner's spades are probably not a genuine suit, but there can be no harm in raising, as he is prepared to go to five clubs.

The lead
West begins with king and ace of diamonds, South ruffing. How should South plan the play?

Preliminary analysis
Declarer can count four top tricks in clubs, four in spades, and the ace of hearts. Two ruffs will make up the total of eleven tricks. It looks easy, but there is a small trap.

It looked like the easiest of reverse dummies. Having ruffed a diamond at trick two, South played ace and another club, ruffed a diamond, and attempted to enter dummy with the king of spades. Now disaster struck. East ruffed the spade and led a heart. The best that South could do was give up a heart to the king, conceding one down.

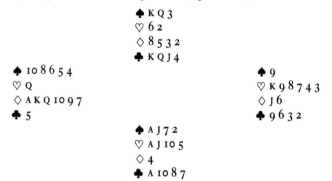

```
                    ♠ K Q 3
                    ♡ 6 2
                    ◇ 8 5 3 2
                    ♣ K Q J 4
♠ 10 8 6 5 4                              ♠ 9
♡ Q                                       ♡ K 9 8 7 4 3
◇ A K Q 10 9 7                            ◇ J 6
♣ 5                                       ♣ 9 6 3 2
                    ♠ A J 7 2
                    ♡ A J 10 5
                    ◇ 4
                    ♣ A 10 8 7
```

It was unlucky – or at any rate unexpected – to find West with five spades as well as six diamonds, but South's timing was wrong. Most players know that on a crossruff hand winners in the side suits should be cashed before the crossruff begins. The same principle should have been applied here. South should enter dummy with a spade at trick three, before East has had a chance to discard on the third diamond. The type of mistake that declarer made usually goes unpunished, but here it did not.

Dealer, West   N–S vulnerable

♠ 9 6 5 2
♥ Q 7 4
♦ 8 5 2
♣ Q 9 4

♠ K led

♠ —
♥ A K J 10 8 2
♦ A 9 4
♣ A K J 10

The bidding

South	West	North	East
—	1 ♠	pass	pass
2 ♠	pass	2NT (1)	pass
3 ♥	pass	4 ♥	pass
5 ♣ (2)	pass	6 ♥ (3)	pass
pass	pass		

Final contract – Six Hearts

(1) North has an awkward call, as he has no guard in spades and no other four-card suit. However, partner is unlikely to raise no trumps unless he has some strength in spades, so it is better to misrepresent the spade holding than to bid a non-existent suit.

(2) Whether South should make a slam try is doubtful, but he expects five hearts to be reasonably safe.

(3) As the bidding has gone, North has fair values.

The lead
West leads the king of spades. How should South plan the play?

Preliminary analysis
If trumps are 2–2 declarer will have no problems: he can discard a diamond from dummy on the fourth club and lose just one diamond. But suppose the trumps are 3–1: is there a plan to take care of that?

An unthinking player would ruff the spade lead and draw two rounds of trumps. See where that leads.

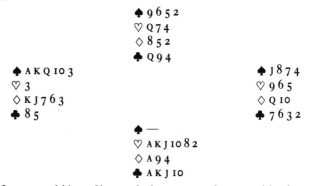

                        ♠ 9 6 5 2
                        ♡ Q 7 4
                        ◇ 8 5 2
                        ♣ Q 9 4
    ♠ A K Q 10 3   ♠ J 8 7 4
    ♡ 3   ♡ 9 6 5
    ◇ K J 7 6 3   ◇ Q 10
    ♣ 8 5   ♣ 7 6 3 2
                        ♠ —
                        ♡ A K J 10 8 2
                        ◇ A 9 4
                        ♣ A K J 10

After ace and king of hearts declarer enters dummy with a low club and leads a diamond, hoping to duck the trick into West's hand. This proves impossible, and when East takes his diamond trick he plays a third trump, killing the possibility of a diamond ruff.

It is in order to draw one round of trumps, but South's next play should be a low diamond. Say that the defenders win and return a diamond. South draws a second trump, then takes four rounds of clubs, discarding a diamond from dummy. East is obliged to follow suit, and then the losing diamond is ruffed.

Dealer, South   *Game all*

♠ A Q 3
♡ J 7
◇ A Q J 9 8 2
♣ 10 8

♣ 6 led

♠ K 9 7 4 2
♡ K 10
◇ K 3
♣ A J 5 2

The bidding

South	West	North	East
1 ♠	pass	2 ◇	pass
2NT	pass	3 ♠ (1)	pass
4 ♠	pass	pass	pass

Final contract – Four Spades

(1) It looks natural to show the support for spades, but North might have reflected that if his partner held the king of diamonds 3NT could hardly go wrong, and if he did not hold this card he would surely have a double stop in the other suits. There was a good case for raising to 3NT.

The lead

West leads the 6 of clubs, East plays the queen and South wins with the ace. How should South plan the play?

Preliminary analysis

When the dummy goes down, South sees that 3NT would have been unbeatable and that six spades or 6NT would be a good contract, though difficult to reach. Four spades looks easy, unless the trumps are going to be awkward. South has to consider the best order of play in the trump suit.

South decided, quite rightly, that to attempt to ruff a club would be clumsy and that he must play to run the diamond suit. When he led a spade to dummy West played the 8.

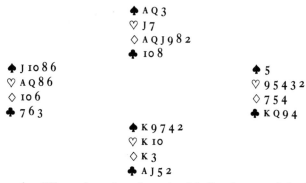

```
              ♠ A Q 3
              ♡ J 7
              ◇ A Q J 9 8 2
              ♣ 10 8
♠ J 10 8 6                        ♠ 5
♡ A Q 8 6                         ♡ 9 5 4 3 2
◇ 10 6                            ◇ 7 5 4
♣ 7 6 3                           ♣ K Q 9 4
              ♠ K 9 7 4 2
              ♡ K 10
              ◇ K 3
              ♣ A J 5 2
```

Muttering 'We ought to have been in six', South covered the 8 of spades with the queen and followed with the ace, expecting to pick up the spade suit without loss.

When East discarded the 2 of hearts on the second spade, the picture changed. In danger of losing a club, a spade and two hearts, South took a heart discard on the third diamond. West ruffed and led his last trump. This left South with two club losers in addition to a heart and a trump.

On hands of this type, where dummy has a strong side suit, it is essential to keep a high trump as an entry card. After winning the first spade in dummy South should return to the king. When he sees that the spades are not breaking he can turn to diamonds. On the third round he discards a heart and West ruffs. The defence then make one club and one heart, but that is all.

Dealer, South   *Game all*

♠ 3
♡ Q 9 6
◇ A J 9 7 4
♣ A K 8 3

♣ Q led

♠ A K 9 6 4 2
♡ A K J 10
◇ 3
♣ 6 4

The bidding

South	West	North	East
1 ♠	pass	2 ◇	pass
2 ♡	pass	3 ♣	pass
3 ♠	pass	4 ♡	pass
5 ♡ (1)	pass	6 ♡	pass
pass	pass		

Final contract – Six Hearts

(1) South has given a picture of his 6–4 distribution but has not so far expressed his strength. As the hearts, for a four-card suit, are strong, he chooses this suit for his slam try.

The lead
West leads the queen of clubs. The king is played from dummy and East follows with the 2. How should South plan the play?

Preliminary analysis
There are two possible lines of play – to set up the spades or to crossruff. Assuming that the five side winners can be safely cashed, South will need to make all the trumps separately to win twelve tricks, and that may not be possible. If neither major suit breaks worse than 4–2, can declarer establish the spades and retain control?

To make the contract on a crossruff, South will need to cash five winners in the side suits and ruff three times in dummy. This line will fail if East is able to overruff dummy's 6 of hearts on the third round of spades.

What are the chances, then, of drawing trumps and setting up the spades? Can it be done if both suits break 4–2, East having the doubleton spade?

♠ 3
♡ Q 9 6
◇ A J 9 7 4
♣ A K 8 3

♠ Q 10 8 5   ♠ J 7
♡ 7 2   ♡ 8 5 4 3
◇ K 8 6   ◇ Q 10 5 2
♣ Q J 10 5   ♣ 9 7 2

♠ A K 9 6 4 2
♡ A K J 10
◇ 3
♣ 6 4

Suppose declarer begins with ace, king and another spade, ruffing with the 9 of hearts. The spades are not yet established, so he returns to hand with a trump and leads another spade. If he ruffs this trick the hand disintegrates because he can get back to hand only by ruffing one of the minor suits. Nor will it help, as the cards lie, to refrain from ruffing the fourth spade, because East will have had the opportunity to discard two clubs and a club ruff will follow.

The most accurate line is to give up the second, or even the first, round of spades. Then one spade is ruffed with a high trump and the rest of the hand is under control.

Dealer, South   Love all

♠ 10 6 5 3
♡ J 5
◇ A 8 6 3
♣ A 8 2

♠ 9 led

♠ A K 4 2
♡ A Q 10
◇ J 2
♣ K 7 4 3

The bidding

South	West	North	East
1 ♣	pass	1 ◇	pass
1 ♠	pass	2 ♠	pass
2NT	pass	4 ♠ (1)	pass
pass	pass		

Final contract – Four Spades

(1) North has a fairly close choice between 3NT and four spades. He bids game in the suit because his hand lacks the sort of intermediates that are useful at notrumps.

The lead

West leads the 9 of spades, East plays the 7 and South wins with the king. How should he plan the play?

Preliminary analysis

It looks as though the trumps are 3–2, East holding Q J 7. To avoid losing a trick in each suit, declarer needs either a successful heart finesse or, if this fails, to discard a club from dummy on the third heart and lose no club trick. However, the opponents have made a good start with a trump lead and there may be entry problems.

The full hand was:

```
                    ♠ 10 6 5 3
                    ♡ J 5
                    ◇ A 8 6 3
                    ♣ A 8 2
♠ 9 8                                    ♠ Q J 7
♡ K 8 4 3                                ♡ 9 7 6 2
◇ K 7 5                                  ◇ Q 10 9 4
♣ Q 9 6 5                                ♣ J 10
                    ♠ A K 4 2
                    ♡ A Q 10
                    ◇ J 2
                    ♣ K 7 4 3
```

After taking the first spade, South crossed to the ace of clubs and took the heart finesse. West won and led a second trump, the jack forcing the ace. South discarded a club from dummy on the third round of hearts, then played king of clubs and ruffed a club.

South would have been home now if East had overruffed, but East did not oblige. When declarer played a low diamond from dummy East hopped up with the queen and drew a third round of trumps. This left South with a losing club and no trump in dummy.

It was good defence, but South should have realised that East was the danger hand and should have attacked his possible entry first. At trick two declarer must duck a diamond. The defenders play a second round of trumps. South crosses to dummy and takes the heart finesse, losing to the king. The difference is that the decks are now cleared for South to go from hand to hand without letting East in to draw two trumps for one.

Dealer, South   *Love all*

           ♠ J 10 8 3
           ♡ —
           ◇ A K 3
           ♣ J 9 7 4 3 2

♠ K led

           ♠ —
           ♡ A K 7 6 5 4
           ◇ J 10 9 7 5 4
           ♣ 10

The bidding

South	West	North	East
1 ♡ (1)	dble	pass (2)	1 ♠
2 ◇	2 ♠	3 ◇	3 ♠
4 ◇	4 ♠	dble	pass
5 ◇ (3)	dble	pass	pass
pass			

Final contract – Five Diamonds doubled

(1) There is no 'correct' opening on a hand of this type. Some players would pass, hoping to make an effective entry later, some would try an unorthodox pre-empt of four hearts.

(2) Here, again, there are alternatives, but the best plan probably is to pass and see how the bidding develops.

(3) This may turn out to be the wrong decision, but most players would do the same.

The lead

West leads the king of spades. How should South plan the play?

Preliminary analysis

Obviously South must aim to get the hearts going. At the same time, he must avoid losing trump control; and he must consider whether there is any point in discarding a club on the opening lead, instead of ruffing.

On some hands of this type it is good play to discard on the first trick, instead of ruffing, the object being to restrict the communications between the defending hands. However, there is no reason to do that here and a trump switch would be unwelcome.

South ruffs the opening lead, therefore, and the next problem is whether to ruff low hearts or to start by playing off the ace and king. As a rule, it is right to cash the top winners first. All follow to the ace and king of hearts, and West follows to the third round as well, the full hand being:

```
                    ♠ J 10 8 3
                    ♡ —
                    ◇ A K 3
                    ♣ J 9 7 4 3 2
   ♠ A K 4 2                         ♠ Q 9 7 6 5
   ♡ Q 10 8                          ♡ J 9 3 2
   ◇ Q 8 6                           ◇ 2
   ♣ A Q 8                           ♣ K 6 5
                    ♠ —
                    ♡ A K 7 6 5 4
                    ◇ J 10 9 7 5 4
                    ♣ 10
```

This is the critical point. Suppose that South ruffs the third heart with the 3 of diamonds, cashes the ace of diamonds, and returns to hand with a spade ruff to trump the fourth heart. By the time he has ruffed the next spade he will be down to J 10 of diamonds alone, and if he tries to break the suit 2–2 he will make only one more trick.

There is quite a simple way to keep control. After ruffing the spade lead and cashing the top hearts, South ruffs a heart with the king of diamonds, comes back to hand with a spade ruff, and trumps the next heart with the ace of diamonds. Then he can come off the table with a low trump instead of having to shorten his hand again. The defence makes just the queen of diamonds and the ace of clubs.

Dealer, East   *E–W vulnerable*

♠ A 7 6
♡ Q 8 5 4
◇ K 9
♣ K 10 7 4

♡ J led

♠ K 8 4 3 2
♡ 3
◇ Q 7 6
♣ A Q J 8

The bidding

South	West	North	East
—	—	—	1 ♡
dble	pass	2 ♡ (1)	pass
2 ♠	pass	2NT	pass
3 ♣	pass	3 ♠ (2)	pass
4 ♠	pass	pass	pass

Final contract – Four Spades

(1) The response in the opponent's suit is forcing for at least two rounds and is preferable to a plunge into 3NT.

(2) North has given a good picture by now – a useful hand with a stop in hearts and three-card support for spades.

The lead

West leads the jack of hearts. As there may be a chance to block the suit, declarer plays the queen from dummy. East wins with the king and follows with the 10, which South ruffs. How should he plan the play?

Preliminary analysis

South has three top losers – a spade, a heart and a diamond. His problem is how to take care of the third round of diamonds.

The declarer seems to be in a dilemma. If he draws two rounds of trumps before touching the diamonds, East, when he comes in with the ace of diamonds, may be able to draw a third trump, preventing any ruff. On the other hand, if South plays a diamond at once, or after drawing just one round of trumps, East will play a third heart and West may score a damaging overruff. Thus either line of play will fail when East has three trumps, as here:

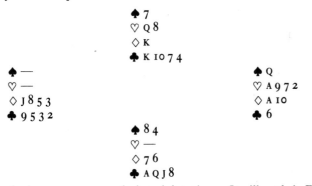

The solution lies in a combination of avoidance play and reverse dummy. South takes two rounds of spades, then leads the 9 of diamonds from the table. East cannot gain by going up with the ace, so he plays low. The position is now:

```
              ♠ 7
              ♡ Q 8
              ◇ K
              ♣ K 10 7 4
♠ —                        ♠ Q
♡ —                        ♡ A 9 7 2
◇ J 8 5 3                  ◇ A 10
♣ 9 5 3 2                  ♣ 6
              ♠ 8 4
              ♡ —
              ◇ 7 6
              ♣ A Q J 8
```

South plays ace, queen, and a low club to the 10. It will not help East to ruff at any point, so we will say that he discards. Declarer then ruffs a heart and plays a fourth club to the king. If East again declines to ruff, South leads the last heart and makes the tenth trick with his remaining trump.

Dealer, South   E–W vulnerable

♠ K Q 7 6 3
♥ J 10 7 4
♦ —
♣ K 10 5 3

♥ 3 led

♠ A 8 4 2
♥ A K Q 5
♦ K J 9 8 3
♣ —

The bidding

South	West	North	East
1 ♦	pass	1 ♠	pass
3 ♥	pass	4 ♥	pass
4 ♠	pass	5 ♦ (1)	pass
6 ♥ (2)	pass	pass	pass

Final contract – Six Hearts

(1) One of the rare occasions when it is safe to cue-bid a suit bid by partner. As hearts and spades have both been vigorously supported, North cannot possibly want to play in five diamonds.

(2) South chooses to play in hearts because from his point of view partner may hold the ace of diamonds and he may want to establish the suit by ruffing, without expending valuable trumps.

The lead
West leads the 3 of hearts. How should South plan the play?

Preliminary analysis
It is one of those hands where there seem to be no losers, yet it is not easy to negotiate twelve tricks. After the trump lead there is no possibility of obtaining three diamond ruffs. The tricks in sight, assuming a reasonable break in both majors, are four top trumps, five spades and two ruffs. South must somehow find a trick in the minor suits.

Hoping to establish tricks in diamonds, South won the trump lead in hand, ruffed a diamond, returned to the king of hearts and ruffed another diamond. Then he returned to the ace of spades and drew the last trump.

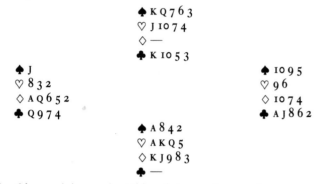

<pre>
                    ♠ K Q 7 6 3
                    ♡ J 10 7 4
                    ◇ —
                    ♣ K 10 5 3
   ♠ J   ♠ 10 9 5
   ♡ 8 3 2   ♡ 9 6
   ◇ A Q 6 5 2   ◇ 10 7 4
   ♣ Q 9 7 4   ♣ A J 8 6 2
                    ♠ A 8 4 2
                    ♡ A K Q 5
                    ◇ K J 9 8 3
                    ♣ —
</pre>

South's remaining cards at this point were three spades, one trump, and K J 9 of diamonds. Dummy's fifth spade would provide one discard but South still needed a trick from diamonds. As West still held ◇ A Q 6, this trick was not forthcoming whether declarer tried to bring down the ace or pin the queen by leading the king.

It was right to play on diamonds, but declarer failed to realize the potential of the K J 9 8. If he can find two diamond honours on his left (an even chance) he can establish a diamond trick by force.

After taking the first trick in hand, South should lead the 8 of diamonds and run it, losing to the 10 as the cards lie. East will probably lead a second trump. South wins and leads the king of diamonds, which West must cover. Dummy ruffs, and after a spade to the ace declarer leads the jack of diamonds, letting it run if West does not cover; then he ruffs a low diamond, returns to hand with a club ruff, and draws the last trump. He has only one diamond left, and this goes on the fifth spade.

Dealer, North   N–S vulnerable

♠ K J 9 7 4 2
♡ —
◊ A K J 9 4
♣ 7 6

♡ A led

♠ 5
♡ 9 7 3
◊ 10 7 5
♣ A K Q J 10 4

The bidding

South	West	North	East
—	—	1 ♠	pass
2 ♣	pass	2 ◊	2 ♡
3 ♣	3 ♡	3 ♠	pass
4 ♣	pass	5 ♣ (1)	pass
pass	pass		

Final contract – Five Clubs

(1) North has bid his own suits twice and the only question is whether the void and the two trumps will provide adequate support.

The lead
West leads the ace of hearts and dummy ruffs. How should South plan the play?

Preliminary analysis
If South draws trumps and takes the diamond finesse he will make twelve tricks or nine (losing a diamond, two hearts and a spade). He has to find a way that will improve his chances of making eleven tricks.

The simplest line is to cash the ace of diamonds, then draw trumps and stake all on the diamond finesse.

A low spade from the table at trick two would be a slight improvement. A weak player in East's position, holding the ace of spades but not the queen, might go up with the ace. This would create additional chances.

The other possibility is to lead the jack of diamonds from dummy at trick two. This wins the contract whenever the diamonds are 3–2.

```
                    ♠ K J 9 7 4 2
                    ♡ —
                    ◇ A K J 9 4
                    ♣ 7 6
    ♠ A 10 8 3                        ♠ Q 6
    ♡ A J 6 2                         ♡ K Q 10 8 5 4
    ◇ 8 2                             ◇ Q 6 3
    ♣ 9 5 2                           ♣ 8 3
                    ♠ 5
                    ♡ 9 7 3
                    ◇ 10 7 5
                    ♣ A K Q J 10 4
```

When South ruffs the heart and leads the jack of diamonds, the best the defence can do is take the queen of diamonds and the ace of spades; if, instead, East forces the dummy with a heart, South can come to hand with the 10 of diamonds.

This line of play would fail, it is true, if West had Q x x x in diamonds, while the simple finesse would win twelve tricks. The fact that the opponents did not go beyond three hearts is a slight indication (apart from normal probabilities) that their hands are comparatively balanced.

Dealer, North   *Game all*

♠ 2
♡ A J 10 7 5
♢ 7 4 2
♣ K 7 3 2

◇ K led

♠ A K J 8 6 3
♡ K Q 9 8
♢ A 5
♣ 10

The bidding

South	West	North	East
—	—	pass	pass
1 ♠	2 ♣	dble (1)	pass
3 ♡ (2)	pass	5 ♡	pass
6 ♡	pass	pass	pass

Final contract – Six Hearts

(1) This was a negative, or 'sputnik', double, showing general values.

(2) As a sputnik double usually reflects length in the other major, South jumps in hearts; his alternative was a cue-bid of three clubs.

The lead

West leads the king of diamonds and the dummy is not exactly what South was hoping to see. After winning with the ace of diamonds, how should he continue?

Preliminary analysis

Clearly South needs to get the spades going. Five tricks in spades plus (altogether) six in hearts will be enough, or four tricks in spades plus seven in hearts. In other words, he wants spades to be 3–3 and hearts 3–1, or spades 4–2 and hearts 2–2. The problem is how to combine the chances in the major suits.

This contract will be easy to make if spades are 3–3 and hearts 3–1, or if spades are 4–2 and hearts 2–2. Declarer must be sure to give himself both chances. The wrong way to play is to begin with ace of spades and a spade ruff. Observe the effect of that:

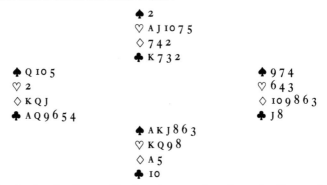

South wins the diamond lead, cashes ace of spades and ruffs a spade, then returns to hand with the king of hearts. Though it may not be evident from the diagram, he is in a dilemma now, for this reason:

(a) If he ruffs another spade (unnecessarily, as the cards lie) and draws trumps, he will be a trick short, because, while he can discard diamonds on the remaining spades, there will be no trump left in dummy.

(b) If he draws a second round of trumps, and it turns out that hearts are 2–2 and spades 4–2, he will not be able to return to hand quickly when he has taken the second ruff in spades.

Better timing saves declarer from the guess. He must clarify the position in spades by leading ace, king and another. As the cards lie, he brings down the queen and can draw the trumps. If, on the other hand, it turns out that spades are 4–2, with the queen still out, South can return to hand with a trump, ruff another spade, and still make the contract when trumps are 2–2.

Really, it is just a problem in communications. When spades are 4–2 and hearts 2–2, the first two rounds of trumps are both needed for entry purposes.

Dealer, South   *Love all*

         ♠ 4 3 2
         ♡ Q 9
         ◇ 10 8 6 4
         ♣ A K Q 9

♠ 6 led

         ♠ A 10 8 7 5
         ♡ A 5 3
         ◇ A
         ♣ J 7 6 2

The bidding

South	West	North	East
1 ♠	pass	2 ♣	pass
3 ♣	pass	3 ♠ (1)	pass
4 ♠	pass	pass	pass

Final contract – Four Spades

(1) A player who opens one spade and raises two clubs to three clubs will always hold five spades, so it is safe to give a delayed raise with these moderate trumps.

The lead

West leads the 6 of spades, East plays the queen, and South lets this hold. East follows with the king of spades; South wins and West plays the 9. How should South continue?

Preliminary analysis

Declarer has lost just one trump so far and clearly he must lose another trump and a trick in hearts. The only worry is the third heart. Can he take care of that safely?

South, at the table, led a heart to the queen at trick three. East won with the king and, to the declarer's dismay, produced the jack of spades. This left South with a certain loser in hearts.

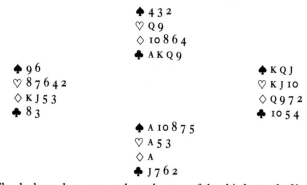

The declarer does not need to take care of the third round of hearts: he can simply ignore it. After winning the second trump he can lay down his cards and claim the contract. The play is: ace of diamonds, club to ace, ruff a diamond, club to king, ruff a diamond, club to queen, ruff a diamond. It won't matter if he is overruffed at any point, as there will still be a trump in dummy for the third heart.

The sight of the 4 3 2 of trumps on the table does not suggest a reverse dummy hand, but in a sense this was.

Dealer, South Game all

        ♠ A K J 10 6
        ♡ 5
        ◇ A 8 5 3
        ♣ Q 6 2

◇ 10 led

        ♠ 9 4
        ♡ A 10 8
        ◇ J 2
        ♣ A K 10 5 4 3

The bidding

South	West	North	East
1 ♣	pass	1 ♠	pass
2 ♣	pass	3 ◇ (1)	pass
3 ♡	pass	4 ♣	pass
6 ♣	pass	pass	pass

Final contract – Six Clubs

(1) After opener has rebid his clubs, the North hand looks strong. As two diamonds would be forcing in most systems, the jump to three diamonds indicates support for clubs and slam interest.

The lead
West leads the 10 of diamonds. How should South plan the play?

Preliminary analysis
Assuming that clubs are not worse than 3–1, declarer can count on six club tricks, two top spades, and two red aces. That is ten tricks already, at least one heart ruff is available, and there is a good suit of spades to be established. It is just a question of how to avoid losing a diamond and a spade or a diamond and a trump.

Show this hand to a group of players who have not seen something like it before, and the popular answer will be: Go up with the ace of diamonds, cash ace and king of clubs; if there is still a trump out, play ace, king and jack of spades, discarding a diamond if the queen has not appeared. This line does not work when East has four spades to the queen and West has J x x of clubs:

```
                    ♠ A K J 10 6
                    ♡ 5
                    ◇ A 8 5 3
                    ♣ Q 6 2
    ♠ 7 3                             ♠ Q 8 5 2
    ♡ K J 7 6 3 2                     ♡ Q 9 4
    ◇ 10 9                            ◇ K Q 7 6 4
    ♣ J 9 8                           ♣ 7
                    ♠ 9 4
                    ♡ A 10 8
                    ◇ J 2
                    ♣ A K 10 5 4 3
```

After a diamond to the ace, two top clubs and two top spades, South leads the jack of spades from dummy. Whether East plays low or puts on the queen, South must lose two more tricks.

The winning play is unexpected. After all have followed to the ace of clubs declarer plays ace, king and jack of spades. If East plays low, South throws a diamond, and the defence can take only the jack of clubs. There are two entries to dummy and the fifth spade can be established.

And if East covers the jack of spades? Then South ruffs high, leads a club to the queen, and plays the good spades, losing only to the jack of clubs.

Not convinced? Then play it through again.

Dealer, South   *Game all*

♠ J 4 3
♡ 6 5 3
◇ A K 8 2
♣ A 7 6

♣ K led

♠ A K Q 10 9
♡ A J 10 8
◇ 7
♣ 9 3 2

The bidding

South	West	North	East
1 ♠	pass	2 ◇	pass
2 ♡	pass	3 ♣ (1)	pass
3 ♠	pass	4 ♠	pass
pass	pass		

Final contract – Four Spades

(1) The bid of the fourth suit is more flexible than a jump to game in spades. It says to partner, 'If you hold a bolster in clubs we might be better off in 3NT.'

The lead

West leads the king of clubs. As he intends to discard a club on the high diamonds, South does not hold off. On the ace of clubs East drops the 5. How should South plan the play?

Preliminary analysis

The contract looks easy, but a count of tricks reveals that there are only nine on top. The tenth trick will presumably come from hearts, and the question is how to manage this suit.

Clearly South must take his club discard at once, playing off ace and king of diamonds. He may then decide that, while in dummy, he must take the first of two finesses in hearts. That line will fail if West has all the hearts, as in this lay-out:

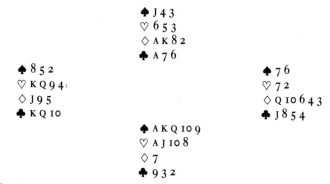

♠ J 4 3
♡ 6 5 3
◇ A K 8 2
♣ A 7 6

♠ 8 5 2
♡ K Q 9 4
◇ J 9 5
♣ K Q 10

♠ 7 6
♡ 7 2
◇ Q 10 6 4 3
♣ J 8 5 4

♠ A K Q 10 9
♡ A J 10 8
◇ 7
♣ 9 3 2

South wins with the ace of clubs, takes his discard on the second diamond, and finesses the jack of hearts. West wins, cashes the queen of clubs, and leads a third round, which South ruffs. After three rounds of trumps, finishing in dummy, declarer finesses the 10 of hearts. West wins again and exits with a diamond. Declarer has lost three tricks and must still lose the fourth round of hearts.

Unlucky! But a declarer who plays in this fashion has been led from the straight path by the J 10 of hearts. If South had held ♡ A x x x he would have seen the right play at once: after taking the club discard, play ace of hearts and another. The best the defence can do is lead a trump. South wins and plays a third round of hearts. Whatever happens, he cannot be prevented from scoring his tenth trick by way of a ruff with the jack of spades.

Dealer, South   *Love all*

♠ A 9 6 2
♡ 6
◇ A 10 9 5
♣ 10 7 4 3

♠ K led

♠ 7 5
♡ A 9 5
◇ K J 8 6 4
♣ A K 5

The bidding

South	West	North	East
1 ◇	dble	redble	1 ♡
pass (1)	pass	2 ◇	pass
3 ♣	pass	4 ◇	pass
5 ◇	pass	pass	pass

Final contract – Five Diamonds

(1) South can pass for the moment because his partner, having redoubled, is pledged to bid again if West passes.

The lead
West leads the king of spades. How should South plan the play?

Preliminary analysis
After this lead, South must expect to lose a spade and a club, so his problem is to avoid a trump loser. Must he guess, or can he do better?

As West doubled the opening one diamond, the simple line is to play him for a singleton trump. However, the hand may be like this:

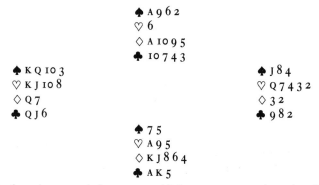

Declarer has a good chance to avoid the trump guess altogether. He should duck the first spade, win the continuation, and proceed as follows: spade ruff, club ace, ace of hearts and heart ruff, club to king, heart ruff. The position is now:

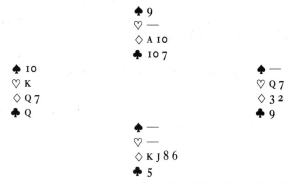

Declarer plays a spade from the table. When East discards on this trick, South is home for sure. He ruffs and exits with a club, end-playing the opponents to avoid a guess in the trump suit.

Dealer, South   *Love all*

♠ K Q 4
♡ A J 10 5
◇ J 10 8
♣ 10 4 2

♣ K led

♠ A 8 5 3
♡ 7 4
◇ A K Q 9 5 3
♣ 6

The bidding

South	West	North	East
1 ◇	pass	1 ♡	pass
1 ♠	pass	2 ♣ (1)	pass
3 ◇ (2)	pass	5 ◇	pass
pass	pass		

Final contract – Five Diamonds

(1) This bid of the fourth suit keeps the bidding alive when no good natural call is available. In particular, North wants to know if the opener has a guard in clubs and can bid notrumps.

(2) With about seven playing tricks, South must make a forward move after his partner's bid of the fourth suit.

The lead
West leads the king of clubs and follows with the ace. How should South plan the play?

Preliminary analysis
There are ten tricks on top and the chances for an eleventh include a 3–3 break in spades, a combination finesse in hearts, or a 2–2 break in trumps, which would allow South to ruff the fourth spade if necessary. There are also squeeze possibilities, should the same hand control the fourth round of both major suits. There may even be a stronger line than any of these.

The numerous chances can to some extent be combined. For example, South can ruff the second club, finesse the 10 of hearts, win a trump return and play ace and another heart. He wins if the second heart honour comes down, if trumps are 2–2, or spades 3–3, or if the fourth heart and fourth spade are in the same hand. However, it is possible for all these chances to fail, as in this diagram:

```
                    ♠ K Q 4
                    ♡ A J 10 5
                    ◇ J 10 8
                    ♣ 10 4 2
   ♠ 9 7 6 2                        ♠ J 10
   ♡ 6 3 2                          ♡ K Q 9 8
   ◇ 6                              ◇ 7 4 2
   ♣ A K J 9 8                      ♣ Q 7 5 3
                    ♠ A 8 5 3
                    ♡ 7 4
                    ◇ A K Q 9 5 3
                    ♣ 6
```

The most reliable line of all is a reverse dummy. South ruffs the second club and leads a heart to the 10 and king. East will probably return a trump. South lets this run to dummy, ruffs a club with a high trump, plays a heart to the ace and ruffs a heart, plays a spade to the queen and ruffs the fourth heart. Then he can draw the remaining trumps with dummy's J 10. He makes three top trumps in dummy, ruffs four times in hand, and has four top winners in the major suits.

Dealer, South   Game all

♠ J
♡ J 4
◇ A Q 9 5
♣ 10 8 7 6 4 2

◇ 2 led

♠ K 9 8 7 6 3
♡ Q 6
◇ 8 7 3
♣ A K

The bidding

South	West	North	East
1 ♠	pass	1NT (1)	pass
2 ♠	pass	pass	pass

Final contract – Two Spades

(1) Not ideal, but better than a sub-standard response of two clubs.

The lead

West leads the 2 of diamonds. Declarer goes in with the queen, which holds, and leads the jack of spades. This is covered by the queen, king and ace. West leads another low diamond and dummy's ace wins, East dropping the 10. How should South continue?

Preliminary analysis

There are five certain losers – two hearts, two spades and a diamond. The only other possible loser is a third trump. Can South take any precautions against this?

It may seem natural to come to hand with the ace of clubs and lead the 7 of spades, hoping to slip this through. This play gave the defenders a chance, which they took.

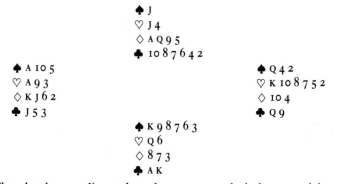

The play began: diamond to the queen, spade jack, covered by queen, king and ace, diamond to ace. When South came to hand with the ace of clubs and led the 7 of spades West alertly went in with the 10 and cashed his king of diamonds. This gave East a chance to discard his second club, and a club ruff followed.

The way to avoid the club ruff is simple but somehow elusive: declarer must cash the second club before leading the 7 of spades.

Dealer, South   Love all

```
              ♠ A 9
              ♡ 7 3
              ◇ A K 8 3
              ♣ A 7 6 4 2
◇ Q led

              ♠ K Q J 7 3
              ♡ A K Q 8 4
              ◇ 6 2
              ♣ J
```

The bidding

South	West	North	East
1 ♠	pass	2 ♣	pass
2 ♡	pass	3 ◇	pass
4 ♡	pass	5 ♠ (1)	pass
6 ♠	pass	pass	pass

Final contract – Six Spades

(1) The jump to five, by-passing a conventional 4NT, conveys the message that all necessary controls are held and that a slam should be on if partner's suits are reasonably strong.

The lead

The queen of diamonds is taken by the ace. Playing with correct technique, South leads a heart to the ace, crosses to the ace of clubs, and leads a second heart from the table, on which East discards a club. How should South continue?

Preliminary analysis

South takes the second heart with the king. He has two heart losers now. The question is whether he should ruff the next heart with the ace of spades or with the 9, risking an overruff.

Declarer may think that if he ruffs one heart with the ace, returns with a club ruff, and ruffs the next heart with the 9, he will be in danger of losing control. But that is a blind spot.

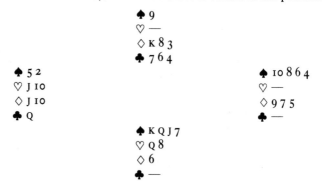

♠ A 9
♡ 7 3
♢ A K 8 3
♣ A 7 6 4 2

♠ 5 2
♡ J 10 6 5 2
♢ Q J 10
♣ Q 9 3

♠ 10 8 6 4
♡ 9
♢ 9 7 5 4
♣ K 10 8 5

♠ K Q J 7 3
♡ A K Q 8 4
♢ 6 2
♣ J

The play begins: diamond to the ace, heart to the ace, club to ace, second heart, on which East discards a club.

If South wins and attempts to ruff the next heart with the 9, East will overruff and return a trump, leaving South with a heart loser.

The right play is to ruff the third heart with the ace of spades, return to hand with a club ruff, and lead the other low heart in this position:

♠ 9
♡ —
♢ K 8 3
♣ 7 6 4

♠ 5 2
♡ J 10
♢ J 10
♣ Q

♠ 10 8 6 4
♡ —
♢ 9 7 5
♣ —

♠ K Q J 7
♡ Q 8
♢ 6
♣ —

If East overruffs the 9 of spades with the 10, South will be in control. And if East declines to overruff? That would be good play in certain similar situations, but here South can make another low trump by ruffing and lose just a trump trick at the finish.

Dealer, South   *Love all*

♠ 10 9 3 2
♡ A 8 4 2
◇ A 7
♣ 7 6 2

♠ K led

♠ 5
♡ K J 3
◇ K Q 5
♣ A K 9 8 4 3

The bidding

South	West	North	East
1 ♣	1 ♠	dble (1)	pass
3 ♣	pass	5 ♣	pass
pass	pass		

Final contract – Five Clubs

(1) A negative double, suggesting initially moderate values, probably with four cards of the other major.

The lead
West leads the king of spades and switches to a diamond. South takes this with the king and plays off ace and king of clubs, West dropping the 5 on the first round and discarding a spade on the second. How should South continue?

Preliminary analysis
All depends now on not losing a heart. South has a dual task – to form an opinion about the lie of the queen and to consider what can be done if West has the queen guarded.

Both to learn more about the distribution and to leave West in sole command of the spades, declarer's first step should be to eliminate spades from the East hand.

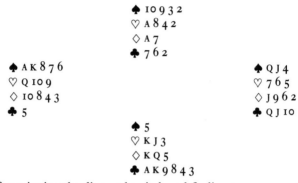

After winning the diamond switch and finding trumps 3–1, South plays a diamond to the ace and ruffs a spade. Then he ruffs the queen of diamonds so that he can play a third spade from dummy.

Having ruffed out East's spades, South lets him take his trump trick. East's best return is a heart. It looks, on all grounds, as though West has the queen, so declarer goes up with the king and plays trumps until he reaches this position:

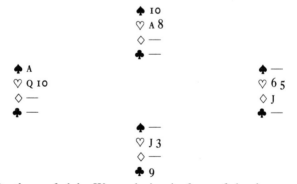

On the 9 of clubs West, playing in front of the dummy, has to unguard the queen of hearts. The squeeze would not work unless East's spades had been eliminated.

Dealer, South   Love all

♠ A K 10
♡ Q 2
◇ A J 4 3
♣ A 8 7 6

◇ K led

♠ Q J 8 7 5
♡ A K J 4 3
◇ 2
♣ Q 5

The bidding

South	West	North	East
1 ♠	pass	3 ♣ (1)	pass
3 ♡	pass	3 ♠	pass
4 ♡ (2)	pass	4NT	pass
5 ◇	pass	6 ◇ (3)	pass
6 ♡ (4)	pass	7 ♠	pass
pass	pass		

Final contract – Seven Spades

(1) North chooses to force in the lowest suit, because this leaves more time for development.

(2) Indicating that he has a good suit and is not minimum.

(3) North wants to make a grand slam try at this point. He chooses the unbid suit because this is unambiguous and also because it leaves partner room to cue-bid in hearts.

(4) Spades are in theory the agreed suit, so the bid of six hearts confirms that South's main strength lies in this suit. It also suggests that South is not unwilling to play in a grand slam.

The lead

West leads the king of diamonds, dummy wins and East plays the 6. How should South plan the play?

Preliminary analysis

A little disappointingly, there are only twelve tricks on top (assuming that hearts are not worse than 4–2). One possibility of a thirteenth is that the queen of diamonds will fall in three rounds. What else is there?

The trap here is to proceed too quickly with a promising line of play. Any experienced declarer would recognize a chance for reverse dummy play: if you can take three diamond ruffs in hand, then draw trumps with dummy's A K 10, you will have enough tricks, barring accidents.

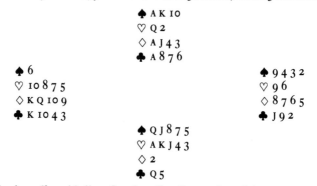

Setting off on this line, South ruffs a diamond at trick two, crosses to the king of spades and ruffs another diamond. He plans then to cross to the ace of spades, ruff a fourth diamond with his last trump, return to ace of clubs, and so forth. This plan fails because, once South has ruffed twice, he must lose a trump trick.

The point that declarer has overlooked when following this sequence is that he can test the trump division before committing himself to the reverse-dummy line. It is right to ruff a diamond at trick two, but then he should draw ace and king of spades.

The trumps do not break, but South has a second string to his bow. He plays off all the hearts and spades. West, having to discard from ◇ Q and ♣ K 10 in front of dummy's ◇ J and ♣ A 8, is caught in a one-way squeeze.

Dealer, South   *Game all*

♠ A K 6 4
♡ A 7
♢ 9 8 3
♣ A K 7 2

♢ K led

♠ Q J 10 9 7 3
♡ 4 2
♢ A J 5
♣ Q 6

The bidding

South	West	North	East
2 ♠ (1)	pass	2NT (2)	pass
3 ♢ (3)	pass	4 ♣	pass
4 ♠	pass	5 ♡	pass
6 ♠ (4)	pass	pass	pass

Final contract – Six Spades

(1) A weak two bid, suggesting 7 to 11 points and a six-card suit.

(2) The only forcing response.

(3) Showing that he has values in diamonds and that his two bid was not a minimum.

(4) South hopes that his queen of clubs will be a decisive card.

The lead

West leads the king of diamonds and East plays the 2. How should South plan the play?

Preliminary analysis

South has eleven solid tricks on top. It is hardly likely that West will present declarer with a second trick in diamonds, so the twelfth trick can come only from a squeeze.

It is well known that, on the majority of occasions, a declarer has a better chance of bringing off a squeeze when he is in a position to win all the remaining tricks but one. On the present hand South had eleven tricks on top and it seemed natural to duck the first diamond, not in the hope of making two tricks with the A J, but to rectify the count for a squeeze. The result was rather sad, for West led a second diamond and East ended the affair by ruffing.

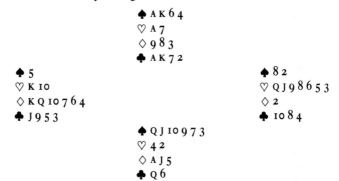

The only chance for a squeeze was to find West with the long clubs as well as the queen of diamonds. South failed to see that, for this squeeze, it would not be necessary to correct the timing. He can take the first diamond and play for this ending:

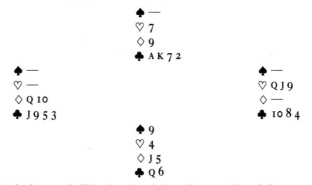

On the last spade West has the choice of unguarding clubs or coming down to the queen of diamonds alone. It is a squeeze-without-the-count, in the sense that a trick is lost after the squeeze card has been played.

Dealer, West   Game all

♠ Q 10 7 4 2
♡ 6
♢ 10 5 3
♣ A Q 7 4

♠ J led

♠ A K 9 8 6 5 3
♡ A Q
♢ A 7
♣ 6 2

The bidding

South	West	North	East
—	pass	pass	3 ♣
4 ♠	pass	5 ♣	pass
5 ♢	pass	5 ♡ (1)	pass
6 ♠	pass	pass	pass

Final contract – Six Spades

(1) Whether North should make another slam suggestion is doubtful, but South would probably go to six in any event.

The lead

West leads the jack of spades and East discards a club. How should West plan the play?

Preliminary analysis

Obviously West is void of clubs. South will probably try for an endplay against East. Can he overcome the strongest defence?

Declarer's first idea will be to ruff a heart and run off all his trumps, reducing to A 7 of diamonds and 6 2 of clubs, with three clubs and a diamond in dummy. But will this be good enough?

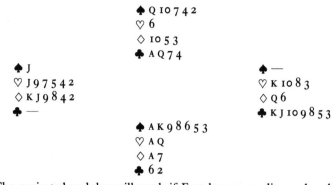

♠ Q 10 7 4 2
♡ 6
◇ 10 5 3
♣ A Q 7 4

♠ J
♡ J 9 7 5 4 2
◇ K J 9 8 4 2
♣ —

♠ —
♡ K 10 8 3
◇ Q 6
♣ K J 10 9 8 5 3

♠ A K 9 8 6 5 3
♡ A Q
◇ A 7
♣ 6 2

The projected endplay will work if East keeps one diamond and three clubs (South will cash the ace of diamonds, then duck a club), or two diamonds and two clubs (South will duck a club). But East, instead, will come down to one heart, one diamond and two clubs.

How can South stop East from wriggling out in this way? By a very pretty stroke. It looks as though the heart finesse is of no value, but it wins the contract because the discard on the ace of hearts enables the declarer to bring off an ending to which there is no defence. When the queen of hearts holds, South discards a diamond on the ace of hearts, then plays ace and another diamond. Whoever wins this trick will be on play – West because he is void in clubs, East because he has the king.

(This hand wandered into the section on squeeze play because South can also make the contract on a squeeze after finessing the queen of hearts; but the play described above is simpler.)

Dealer, West   N–S vulnerable

♠ 6 5 2
♡ A K 3
◇ Q 9 4 2
♣ A 9 2

♡ 9 led

♠ A Q
♡ 10 7 4
◇ A K J 10 8 5
♣ K 4

The bidding

South	West	North	East
—	3 ♠	pass	pass
3NT (1)	pass	4NT (2)	pass
5 ◇	pass	5 ♡ (3)	pass
6 NT	pass	pass	pass

Final contract – 6NT

(1) As a double in the protective position would be for take-out, 3NT is to play.

(2) Not conventional, of course; North simply indicates that a slam should be on if South is not minimum.

(3) North is prepared, if South makes the strong rebid of five spades, to show his ace of clubs as well.

The lead

West leads the 9 of hearts, dummy's king wins, and East drops the 5. How should South plan the play?

Preliminary analysis

There are eleven tricks on top. Declarer would like to be able to throw West in and force a lead away from the king of spades, but even if West has a club holding such as Q x or Q x x it will not be difficult for him to avoid the throw-in. What other chance is there to establish a twelfth trick?

West could be thrown in and forced to lead a spade if he had certain holdings in clubs, but this is a slender chance and declarer's thoughts should turn more to a squeeze. West, no doubt, controls the third round of spades, and it is quite likely that only East can control the third round of hearts. In that case there should be a double squeeze, with clubs as the pivotal suit.

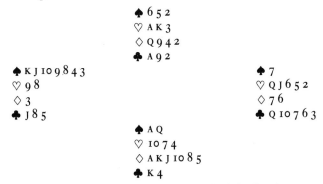

The only problem lies in the timing. In principle, South wants to arrive at a position where he can make all the remaining tricks but one. He needs to 'rectify the count' by losing an early trick. At the same time, he must not destroy one of his menace cards – by ducking a heart or club, for example. The place to give up a trick is in spades!

After winning the first trick with the king of hearts, South plays a spade to the queen and king. West will probably play another heart. South runs off all the diamonds and on the last diamond West will be forced to throw a club, as he must keep a spade in front of dummy. Now the spade is thrown from the table and East, who has to keep the queen of hearts, will probably throw a club as well. Then declarer makes the last three tricks in clubs.

Dealer, South   *Game all*

```
                    ♠ A K
                    ♡ 7 4
                    ◇ Q J 5 4 3 2
                    ♣ K Q J
◇ A led

                    ♠ 9 6 3
                    ♡ A K Q J 10 9
                    ◇ 8
                    ♣ A 8 2
```

The bidding

South	West	North	East
1 ♡	1 ♠	2 ◇	pass
3 ♡	pass	3 ♠	pass
4 ♣	pass	4 ♠ (1)	pass
6 ♡ (2)	pass	pass	pass

Final contract – Six Hearts

(1) Whether North should say more than four hearts at this point is doubtful, but he decides that his spade control may be vital and that five hearts should be safe.

(2) The repeat cue-bid in spades obviously suits South very well.

The lead

West leads the ace of diamonds and switches to a spade. As it may not be safe to ruff the third round of spades, South plays a diamond from dummy. On this trick East discards a spade. South ruffs and plays the ace of hearts, West dropping the 8. How should South continue?

Preliminary analysis

South may regret now that he did not cash two spades and ruff the third round with the 7 of hearts. It may still be safe to lay down the second spade, but is that risk necessary?

West is marked with five diamonds and (from the bidding) at least five spades, so it should be possible to bring pressure to bear on him. In fact, all the elements are present for a ruffing squeeze of the criss-cross variety.

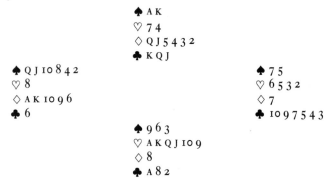

After ace of diamonds and a spade switch South can make the contract by ruffing the third round of spades with the 7 of hearts, but it was more natural to play a diamond from the table, keeping all the entries in dummy. After ruffing the diamond South plays four rounds of trumps, then ace and another club, arriving at this position:

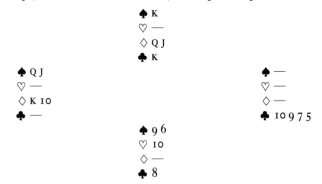

On the king of clubs West is forced to unguard spades or diamonds. In this type of ending declarer must keep one trump in hand and two controlling cards in dummy – in this case the king of spades and the club winner.

Dealer, North   Game all

```
              ♠ A 10 7
              ♡ K J 4
              ◇ A K Q 9 3
              ♣ 8 5
♠ Q led

              ♠ 8 6 4
              ♡ A Q 10 8
              ◇ 8 4
              ♣ A Q 7 3
```

The bidding

South	West	North	East
—	—	1 ◇	pass
1 ♡	pass	3 ♡ (1)	pass
4 ♣	pass	4 ◇	pass
4 ♡	pass	4 ♠ (2)	pass
6 ♡ (3)	pass	pass	pass

Final contract – Six Hearts

(1) The double raise with three trumps is unusual, but the only alternative is an irregular one spade, which might lead to unnecessary confusion.

(2) As South has made a slam try by bidding four clubs, North feels obliged to indicate his spade control. This may be all that his partner wants to hear.

(3) It looks as though the slam will depend on a finesse or on finding a fair break in diamonds.

The lead
West leads the queen of spades. How should South plan the play?

Preliminary analysis
The bidding by both players was on the forward side and South sees that even a 3–3 break in diamonds will produce only eleven tricks. The club finesse will certainly be needed, but it will hardly be possible to ruff two clubs, and keep control of the trump situation.

The hand is a little frustrating. Superficially, a club finesse, a club ruff, and a 4–2 break in diamonds should produce twelve tricks by way of four top trumps, two clubs, a club ruff, spade ace, and four diamonds. The difficulty with this is that, after the ace of spades has been driven out and a club ruff has been taken, it won't be practical (even if trumps are 3–3) to ruff a diamond and return to dummy to make the long diamonds.

A club finesse and one club ruff will provide eleven tricks on top. Suppose the long club and the long diamond are in the same hand? Yes, that's worth looking at. In this diagram East controls both minor suits:

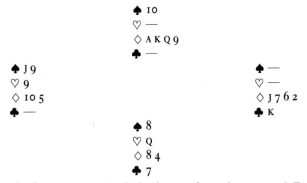

```
                    ♠ A 10 7
                    ♡ K J 4
                    ◇ A K Q 9 3
                    ♣ 8 5
  ♠ Q J 9 3                          ♠ K 5 2
  ♡ 9 6 3 2                          ♡ 7 5
  ◇ 10 5                             ◇ J 7 6 2
  ♣ 10 6 4                           ♣ K J 9 2
                    ♠ 8 6 4
                    ♡ A Q 10 8
                    ◇ 8 4
                    ♣ A Q 7 3
```

To make the timing right for a squeeze, South must duck the opening lead. He wins the spade continuation, finesses the queen of clubs and ruffs the third round. Then he draws trumps, arriving at this position:

```
                    ♠ 10
                    ♡ —
                    ◇ A K Q 9
                    ♣ —
  ♠ J 9                             ♠ —
  ♡ 9                               ♡ —
  ◇ 10 5                            ◇ J 7 6 2
  ♣ —                               ♣ K
                    ♠ 8
                    ♡ Q
                    ◇ 8 4
                    ♣ 7
```

On the last trump a spade is thrown from dummy and East is squeezed.

Dealer, West   *Love all*

♠ K 10 7
♡ A K 5 4
◇ A 4 2
♣ Q 7 3

♣ 8 led

♠ A 9 8 5 3
♡ Q 6
◇ Q J 6
♣ J 10 5

The bidding

South	West	North	East
—	1 ◇	dble	1 ♡
2 ♠	pass	3 ♠	pass
3NT (1)	pass	pass	pass

Final contract – 3NT

(1) South takes the reasonable view that if his partner holds an honour in diamonds 3NT may be easier to make than four spades.

The lead
West leads the 8 of clubs, East plays the 4 and South wins with the jack. How should he continue?

Preliminary analysis
As West is presumably short in hearts, the club lead is probably from length. South has eight tricks on top, assuming that the diamond finesse is right. Where should he go for the ninth?

This hand illustrates one of the most valuable forms of technique in a notrump contract.

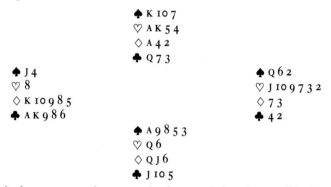

It is dangerous to play on spades because it is quite possible that West's lead of ♣ 8 is from a five-card suit. The best play is to return a club at trick two. If West does not continue clubs it will be safe to duck a spade towards East; and if West plays off his club winners, his partner will be embarrassed when the play reaches this stage:

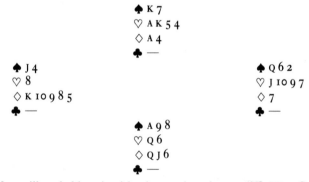

West will probably exit with a heart – it makes no difference. South wins with the queen and two rounds of diamonds are more than East can bear.

Dealer, West   Game all

♠ 9 7 3
♡ 8 7 6 4
◇ A K 2
♣ K 7 6

♠ K led

♠ 4 2
♡ A K J 10 5 2
◇ J 10 4
♣ A 8

The bidding

South	West	North	East
—	1 ♠	pass	pass
3 ♡ (1)	pass	4 ♡	pass
pass	pass		

Final contract – Four Hearts

(1) South is too strong for a simple overcall in the protective position.

The lead

West leads the king of spades and follows with the ace and queen, East playing the 10 on the third round. South lays down the ace of hearts, on which East discards a low club. How should South continue?

Preliminary analysis

What appeared to be a lay-down contract has now become problematical. South has lost two spades and must also lose a trump. Can he improve on the simple finesse in diamonds?

Whatever the situation in diamonds may be, it cannot be wrong to see how the clubs lie by playing off ace, king and another. West, as it happens, follows to all three rounds.

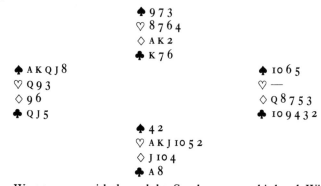

```
                    ♠ 9 7 3
                    ♡ 8 7 6 4
                    ◇ A K 2
                    ♣ K 7 6
♠ A K Q J 8                          ♠ 10 6 5
♡ Q 9 3                              ♡ —
◇ 9 6                               ◇ Q 8 7 5 3
♣ Q J 5                             ♣ 10 9 4 3 2
                    ♠ 4 2
                    ♡ A K J 10 5 2
                    ◇ J 10 4
                    ♣ A 8
```

When West turns up with three clubs, South can count his hand. With four spades and a void East would not have passed the opening one spade, so West must have five. He has shown up with three hearts and (at least) three clubs. That leaves room for at most a doubleton in diamonds.

Instead of finessing the diamond, therefore, South plays off the king of hearts, the ace and king of diamonds, then gives West the lead on the third round of trumps. West has only spades left, so South is able to dispose of his losing diamond while ruffing in the opposite hand.

Dealer, South   *Love all*

♠ Q J 7 5 4 2
♡ —
◊ 10 6 2
♣ K J 6 3

♣ 7 led

♠ A K 10 8 3
♡ 9 4
◊ A 5 4
♣ A 5 2

The bidding

South	West	North	East
1 ♠	3 ♡	4 ♠	5 ♡
pass (1)	pass	5 ♠	pass
pass	pass		

Final contract – Five Spades

(1) A forcing pass; South can rely on his partner, who has given a free raise to four spades, taking action one way or the other.

The lead
West leads the 7 of clubs. How should South plan the play?

Preliminary analysis
The possible losers are two diamonds and a club. The club finesse may be right. Failing that, is there any chance of forcing the opponents to make an unfavourable lead?

First of all, what do you make of the lead? It is unlikely that West, who overcalled with three hearts, will have the length in clubs, and still more unlikely that he would choose to lead from the queen. On the other hand, the lead might well be a singleton. If so, elimination play makes the hand a certainty.

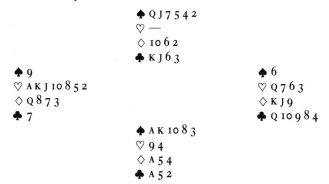

```
                    ♠ Q J 7 5 4 2
                    ♡ —
                    ◇ 10 6 2
                    ♣ K J 6 3
♠ 9                                      ♠ 6
♡ A K J 10 8 5 2                         ♡ Q 7 6 3
◇ Q 8 7 3                                ◇ K J 9
♣ 7                                      ♣ Q 10 9 8 4
                    ♠ A K 10 8 3
                    ♡ 9 4
                    ◇ A 5 4
                    ♣ A 5 2
```

Avoiding what might ineptly be called a 'free' finesse, South plays low from dummy on the club lead and wins with the ace. He ruffs two hearts, drawing trumps in the process, then plays ace and another diamond.

The defenders take their two diamond tricks, but whoever is left on lead is endplayed. If East is on lead he has the choice of a club or conceding a ruff-and-discard, while if West wins the third diamond he has no club to play.

Dealer, South   *Game all*

♠ A 10 7 4
♥ A 3
♦ J 6 2
♣ A 9 8 5

♦ 10 led

♠ 3
♥ Q J 10 9 8 7 4
♦ A K Q
♣ Q 3

The bidding

South	West	North	East
1 ♡	pass	1 ♠	pass
3 ♡	pass	4 ♣ (1)	pass
4 ◇ (2)	pass	6 ♡	pass
pass	pass		

Final contract – Six Hearts

(1) North expects a slam after South's jump rebid, but first he would like to hear that his partner controls the diamonds.

(2) South cannot be sure at this point whether his partner intends to support hearts or has a black two-suiter, but in any event it is natural to indicate that he has tops in diamonds.

The lead

West leads the 10 of diamonds to declarer's ace, East dropping the 4. How should South plan the play?

Preliminary analysis

Unless South is lucky with the hearts, finding West with a singleton king or K x, he will need to develop an extra trick. Assuming that a heart must be lost, what are the chances of escaping a loser in clubs?

Declarer should begin by assuming that he is going to lose a trump trick – otherwise there is no problem. One chance that may occur to him is that if West holds five spades and the king of clubs it may be possible to squeeze him. However, if East wins the heart finesse and returns a club, as he well may, the entry for the squeeze will be removed.

Another, somewhat better, chance may be overlooked. This consists of finding West with not more than three spades, with K x x of hearts, and with the king of clubs. Suppose that this is the distribution:

```
              ♠ A 10 7 4
              ♡ A 3
              ◇ J 6 2
              ♣ A 9 8 5
♠ K 6 2                        ♠ Q J 9 8 5
♡ K 5 2                        ♡ 6
◇ 10 9 8                       ◇ 7 5 4 3
♣ K 10 7 2                     ♣ J 6 4
              ♠ 3
              ♡ Q J 10 9 8 7 4
              ◇ A K Q
              ♣ Q 3
```

The critical play, whether declarer is thinking of the squeeze or the throw-in, comes early. The first move should be a spade to the ace and a spade ruff. Then comes a heart finesse, which holds, and a second heart, on which East shows out. Declarer then ruffs a spade, cashes the remaining top diamonds, and exits with a trump. West, with only clubs left in his hand, is forced to lead away from the king.

You see the importance of taking the spade ruff early on? If South begins with a heart finesse and a heart to the ace, then he cannot eliminate West's spades in time for the endplay.

Dealer, North   Love all

　　　　　　　♠ A Q 5
　　　　　　　♡ A 8
　　　　　　　◇ Q 10 3
　　　　　　　♣ K 9 8 4 2

◇ 6 led

　　　　　　　♠ K 10 8 7 4 2
　　　　　　　♡ Q 5
　　　　　　　◇ 9 4
　　　　　　　♣ A 6 5

The bidding

South	West	North	East
—	—	1 ♣	pass
1 ♠	pass	1 NT (1)	pass
3 ♠	pass	4 ♠	pass
pass	pass		

Final contract – Four Spades

(1) A raise to two spades would not be a mistake, obviously, but as North-South are playing a rebid of 1 NT to show 15–16, 1 NT expresses the hand well.

The lead

West leads the 6 of diamonds and East wins with the jack. He follows with the ace of diamonds, on which West plays the 2, and then switches to the 10 of hearts. How should South plan the play?

Preliminary analysis

South has already lost two tricks, the heart position doesn't look good, and on the surface there is no way to dispose of his third club. If he has no luck with the hearts, can he do anything about the clubs?

ANSWER No. 68

South can be certain of one thing – that the queen of hearts will not win. If East had held the king he would have returned a low diamond at trick two so that his partner could lead a heart through the ace.

Once he has reached this conclusion, South should retain the queen as a possible card of exit. His best chance is that the player who holds the king of hearts will have not more than two clubs.

```
                    ♠ A Q 5
                    ♡ A 8
                    ◇ Q 10 3
                    ♣ K 9 8 4 2
    ♠ 9 3                           ♠ J 6
    ♡ K J 4 3                       ♡ 10 9 7 6 2
    ◇ K 8 7 6 2                     ◇ A J 5
    ♣ 10 7                          ♣ Q J 3
                    ♠ K 10 8 7 4 2
                    ♡ Q 5
                    ◇ 9 4
                    ♣ A 6 5
```

South plays low when the 10 of hearts is led and wins in dummy with the ace. He draws trumps in two rounds, ruffs the third diamond, and cashes ace and king of clubs. Then he plays the queen of hearts. West wins and is forced to lead a red suit, enabling South to ruff in dummy and dispose of his losing club.

Better defence would have beaten the contract. East must attack hearts at trick two, while he still has the ace of diamonds as an entry card.

Dealer, South   *N–S vulnerable*

        ♠ K Q 3
        ♡ K 8 4 .
        ◇ 7 5 2
        ♣ A Q 4 2

◇ 10 led

        ♠ A J 10 9 5
        ♡ —
        ◇ A K 4
        ♣ J 7 6 5 3

The bidding

South	West	North	East
1 ♣	1 ♡	2 ♡ (1)	dble
2 ♠	pass	4 ♣	pass
4 ◇	pass	4 ♠	pass
6 ♣	pass	pass	6 ♡
pass (2)	pass	6 ♠	pass
pass	pass		

Final contract – Six Spades

(1) One advantage of the cue-bid is that if partner holds something like Q x or J x x of hearts he can become the declarer in a notrump contract.

(2) South passes to indicate that there may be a play for six spades. If opponents are going to sacrifice he wants to force them to the highest level.

The lead

West leads the 10 of diamonds. South wins and draws trumps in three rounds, West discarding a low heart. How should South continue?

Preliminary analysis

Five club tricks will be enough for the slam, but if South has to lose a club there will be no obvious way to dispose of the losing diamond.

The club finesse is probably right, but in view of East's bidding the suit is more likely to break 3–1 than 2–2. If a club trick must be lost, there is only one way to avoid losing a diamond as well: West must be forced to lead away from the ace of hearts.

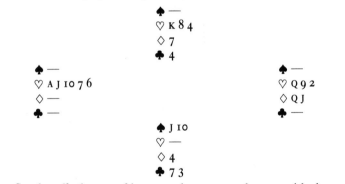

As declarer plans to discard a diamond on the king of hearts, he must take care to retain an entry to dummy. He wins the diamond lead, draws trumps, and leads the 5 of clubs to dummy's queen. Returning to the king of diamonds, he plays the 6 of clubs to the ace and exits with a club. Now West is on play in this position:

♠ —
♡ K 8 4
♢ 7
♣ 4

♠ —
♡ A J 10 7 6
♢ —
♣ —

♠ —
♡ Q 9 2
♢ Q J
♣ —

♠ J 10
♡ —
♢ 4
♣ 7 3

South ruffs the ace of hearts and crosses to dummy with the 4 of clubs, to discard his diamond on the king of hearts.

Dealer, South   *Love all*

♠ A 7 4
♡ K J 10 6 4
◇ 8 5 4
♣ A 6

♡ 2 led

♠ J 10 6
♡ A Q 9 7 3
◇ A Q 9 2
♣ J

The bidding

South	West	North	East
1 ♡	pass	4 ◇ (1)	pass
4 ♡	pass	pass	pass

Final contract – Four Hearts

(1) This is the Swiss convention, in which both four clubs and four diamonds are enlisted to express a fairly strong, as opposed to a pre-emptive, raise to game in partner's major suit. In the variation played here, four diamonds lays stress on the strong trump support.

The lead

West leads a trump, to which his partner follows. South eliminates the clubs by playing ace and another, then draws the second trump. How should he continue?

Preliminary analysis

If the spade honours are in opposite hands, a simple finesse of the 9 of diamonds will be good enough, as West will be obliged either to return a diamond or to open up the spades. But suppose both spades and diamonds lie badly: in that case, can South make a certainty of the contract?

Declarer may think first of playing ace and another spade. That will be good enough whenever West holds one of the spade honours, but it doesn't quite work against this distribution:

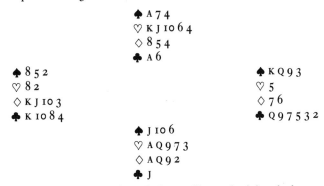

♠ A 7 4
♥ K J 10 6 4
♦ 8 5 4
♣ A 6

♠ 8 5 2
♥ 8 2
♦ K J 10 3
♣ K 10 8 4

♠ K Q 9 3
♥ 5
♦ 7 6
♣ Q 9 7 5 3 2

♠ J 10 6
♥ A Q 9 7 3
♦ A Q 9 2
♣ J

East wins the second spade and plays a diamond, giving declarer no chance.

Another plausible line is to begin with a finesse of the queen of diamonds. West wins and leads a spade to East's queen. When East returns a diamond South can succeed by going up with the ace and exiting with a spade, but that is double dummy.

The sure play is unexpected and difficult to find if you have not seen this type of situation before. South cashes the ace of diamonds at an early stage. When later he leads a low diamond from dummy he covers whatever card East plays. As the cards lie, the 9 is covered by the 10 and West exits with a spade to East's queen. Now if East has a third diamond South must be able to set up a long diamond, and if East, as above, has no more diamonds he must return a spade or a club, to declarer's advantage.

Dealer, North   *Game all*

♠ K 7 4
♡ Q 3
◇ K J 9 4
♣ Q 7 5 2

♠ Q led

♠ —
♡ K J 5 2
◇ A Q 10 7 6 3
♣ A 6 4

The bidding

South	West	North	East
—	—	pass	1 ♠
dble	2 ♠	2NT	pass
3 ◇	pass	4 ◇ (1)	pass
5 ◇	pass	pass	pass

Final contract – Five Diamonds

(1) With no ace and only one stop in spades, North must not insist on a notrump contract when his partner fails to raise 2NT to 3NT.

The lead
West leads the queen of spades and South ruffs. All follow to a round of trumps. How should South continue?

Preliminary analysis
South must lose one trick to the ace of hearts and must avoid losing two clubs. He could play West for the king of clubs, or East for a doubleton K x. If neither of these seems likely, there should be possibilities for an end-play.

The declarer's first idea may be to eliminate the spades and hearts, then lead a low club, intending to duck the trick into East's hand. This line will work if East has something like K J 10 in clubs, but there may well be a defence, as here:

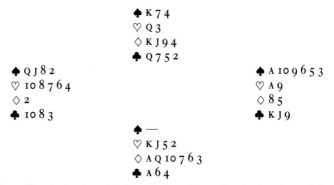

When South, having eliminated the other suits, leads a low club, West must hop up smartly with the 10, preventing a throw-in.

So long as East has the king of clubs, declarer can make sure of the contract by playing a loser-on-loser elimination. After drawing trumps he plays a heart to the queen and ace. He wins the heart return, discards a spade on the jack of hearts, and ruffs the fourth heart, arriving at this position:

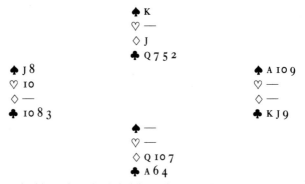

Now the king of spades is led from dummy. East plays the ace and is allowed to hold the trick, South discarding a club.

Dealer, South   Love all

♠ 9 3 2
♡ K 8 6 2
♢ A Q 6
♣ K 10 5

♣ 9 led

♠ A Q
♡ A 10 9 7 4
♢ 8 3
♣ A Q J 2

The bidding

South	West	North	East
1 ♡	pass	3 ♡	pass
4 ♣	pass	4 ◇	pass
4 ♡	pass	5 ♣ (1)	pass
6 ♡	pass	pass	pass

Final contract – Six Hearts

(1) As his raise to three hearts was based on 'tops', North makes another forward move.

The lead

Undeterred by South's bid of four clubs, West leads the 9 of clubs, which runs to the declarer's queen. On a low heart to the king West plays the queen. How should South continue?

Preliminary analysis

After the queen of hearts has appeared on the first round of trumps, there are finesse positions in three suits. South must look for a line of play that will improve on the separate chances.

The best chance of avoiding a loser in the trump suit, considered on its own, is to finesse on the next round rather than play for the drop. South finessed at the table and lost the contract, for the full hand was:

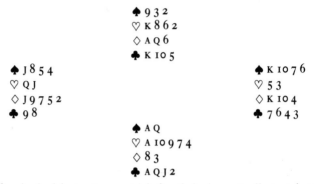

After he had lost a trump trick South had eventually to take the diamond finesse.

The significant point about this hand is that the spade finesse must be taken at some stage, and it should be taken early on. This is because, if it wins, South can make the contract however the trumps and diamonds lie.

After the club lead and the heart to the king declarer finesses the queen of spades. When it holds, he lays down the ace of hearts. If the jack falls the rest is easy. If not, he continues with ace of spades, a club to the king and a spade ruff. The remaining clubs are played off, and if no one has ruffed South exits with a trump. East (if he began with ♡ J x x) has to win the trick and either lead a diamond or concede a ruff-and-discard.

Dealer, South   *Game all*

        ♠ 9 6 5 2
        ♡ J 9
        ◇ Q 7 5 3 2
        ♣ 10 7

♡ K led

        ♠ A K J 10 7 4
        ♡ A 6
        ◇ A J 6
        ♣ K 5

The bidding

South	West	North	East
2 ♠ (1)	pass	2NT (2)	pass
3 ♠	pass	4 ♠	pass
pass	pass		

Final contract – Four Spades

(1) An Acol two bid, forcing for one round.

(2) Though he is prepared to go to four spades, North must make a weakness response on the first round. An immediate raise to three spades would promise an ace, a raise to four spades would show fair values but no ace.

The lead

West leads the king of hearts. How should South plan the play?

Preliminary analysis

Assuming that the spades are not unduly hostile, South has four possible losers – one heart, one diamond and two clubs. He would like to get the diamonds going without allowing East into the lead, but that may not be practicable. Perhaps he can exit in hearts at a timely moment?

Playing with fair confidence, South won the heart lead, drew trumps in two rounds, and exited with a heart, expecting to attract a favourable lead from West. This play was not quite good enough, for the full hand was:

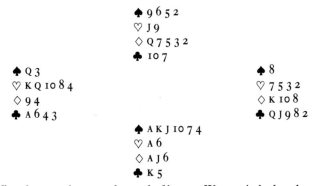

When he won the second round of hearts, West switched to the 9 of diamonds. Dummy played low, East covered with the 10 and South won with the jack. Declarer cashed the ace and followed with the 6. East won and the defenders took two club tricks.

South was a little unlucky to find East with a sure entry in diamonds; if West has 10 x, for example, declarer can let the 10 hold. However, he mistimed the play. He should cross to dummy with a third round of trumps and lead a diamond to the jack. When this holds, he cashes the ace and only then exits with a heart. West wins and must either lead a club or concede a ruff–and–discard.

Dealer, East   *Game all*

    ♠ K 6 4 3
    ♡ Q J 10 8 2
    ◇ A 4
    ♣ 9 3

◇ 8 led

    ♠ A Q 8 7
    ♡ A K 3
    ◇ 9 2
    ♣ A Q J 8

The bidding

South	West	North	East
—	—	—	3 ◇
dble	pass	4 ◇	pass
5 ◇ (1)	pass	5 ♡	pass
5 ♠	pass	6 ♠	pass
pass	pass		

Final contract – Six Spades

(1) To bid simply four spades after partner's strong response hardly seems enough. The only forward-going move available is a further bid of the opponent's suit.

The lead

West leads the 8 of diamonds and declarer wins in dummy. The ace and queen of spades reveal that West began with J 9 x x and has a sure trump trick. On the ace and king of hearts East turns up with another singleton. How should South continue?

Preliminary analysis

It is clear that South can safely discard his losing diamond on the fourth heart. After that, can he improve on a simple club finesse for his contract?

As the play has gone, the slam is a certainty, but an international player missed it.

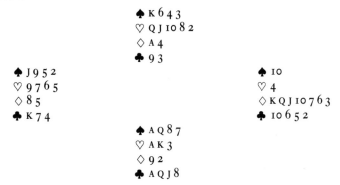

After a diamond to the ace, two rounds of spades and four rounds of hearts, the position is:

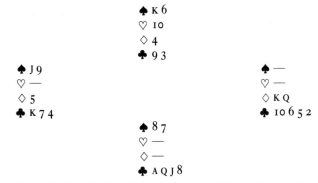

At this point South played the fifth heart. West ruffed and exited with a diamond. South ruffed, drew the last trump, and then had to finesse the club, to go one down.

All he need do in the diagram position is ruff the losing diamond. He returns to the king of spades and leads the fifth heart. West may ruff or discard a club; if he discards he is thrown in with his master trump at trick eleven and forced to lead away from the king of clubs. Somehow, it is easy to miss an end-play when the throw-in card is a trump.

Dealer, South   *Game all*

```
            ♠ K 5
            ♡ A 9 3
            ◇ A J 5 4
            ♣ 7 6 5 4
```

♠ 6 led

```
            ♠ A J 4 3
            ♡ Q 10 8 5
            ◇ K
            ♣ A K Q 9
```

The bidding

South	West	North	East
1 ♣	pass	1 ◇	pass
1 ♡	pass	2NT	pass
3 ♠	pass	4 ♣ (1)	pass
4 ◇	pass	4 ♡	pass
4 ♠	pass	6 ♣ (2)	pass
pass	pass		

Final contract – Six Clubs

(1) As his partner would not have bid three spades, the fourth suit, unless he had ambitions beyond 3NT, North must show his club support at this point.

(2) It looks to North as though the spades and diamonds are under control and there should not be more than one loser in the other two suits.

The lead

West leads the 6 of spades, East plays the queen and South wins with the ace. As the contract is going to be difficult anyway if the trumps are not breaking, South draws two rounds, to which all follow. How should he continue?

Preliminary analysis

South can count four top clubs, one ruff, two diamonds, one heart and, after the lead, three spades. That is eleven tricks. He needs to find an additional trick either from an extra ruff or by developing a second trick in hearts.

It is the sort of hand where there must be many ways of making the contract and declarer's object is to find a safe way. He does not, in fact, need to risk an adverse ruff nor to guess the heart position. Suppose the distribution to be:

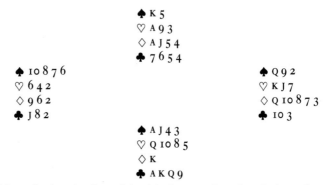

♠ K 5
♡ A 9 3
◇ A J 5 4
♣ 7 6 5 4

♠ 10 8 7 6   ♠ Q 9 2
♡ 6 4 2   ♡ K J 7
◇ 9 6 2   ◇ Q 10 8 7 3
♣ J 8 2   ♣ 10 3

♠ A J 4 3
♡ Q 10 8 5
◇ K
♣ A K Q 9

After winning the first trick with the ace of spades, declarer draws two rounds of trumps, plays a spade to the king, returns with a trump, and cashes the jack of spades, throwing a diamond from dummy. He ruffs the fourth spade and leads a diamond to the king. The position is now:

♠ —
♡ A 9 3
◇ A J
♣ —

♠ —   ♠ —
♡ 6 4 2   ♡ K J 7
◇ 9 6   ◇ Q 10
♣ —   ♣ —

♠ —
♡ Q 10 8 5
◇ —
♣ 9

South plays a low heart to the 9, and whatever East returns will provide the twelfth trick. That's better than guessing!